C-3268   CAREER EXAMINATION SERIES

This is your
PASSBOOK for...

Communication Electrician

Test Preparation Study Guide
Questions & Answers

NATIONAL LEARNING CORPORATION®

COPYRIGHT NOTICE

This book is SOLELY intended for, is sold ONLY to, and its use is RESTRICTED to individual, bona fide applicants or candidates who qualify by virtue of having seriously filed applications for appropriate license, certificate, professional and/or promotional advancement, higher school matriculation, scholarship, or other legitimate requirements of education and/or governmental authorities.

This book is NOT intended for use, class instruction, tutoring, training, duplication, copying, reprinting, excerption, or adaptation, etc., by:

1) Other publishers
2) Proprietors and/or Instructors of "Coaching" and/or Preparatory Courses
3) Personnel and/or Training Divisions of commercial, industrial, and governmental organizations
4) Schools, colleges, or universities and/or their departments and staffs, including teachers and other personnel
5) Testing Agencies or Bureaus
6) Study groups which seek by the purchase of a single volume to copy and/or duplicate and/or adapt this material for use by the group as a whole without having purchased individual volumes for each of the members of the group
7) Et al.

Such persons would be in violation of appropriate Federal and State statutes.

PROVISION OF LICENSING AGREEMENTS – Recognized educational, commercial, industrial, and governmental institutions and organizations, and others legitimately engaged in educational pursuits, including training, testing, and measurement activities, may address request for a licensing agreement to the copyright owners, who will determine whether, and under what conditions, including fees and charges, the materials in this book may be used them. In other words, a licensing facility exists for the legitimate use of the material in this book on other than an individual basis. However, it is asseverated and affirmed here that the material in this book CANNOT be used without the receipt of the express permission of such a licensing agreement from the Publishers. Inquiries re licensing should be addressed to the company, attention rights and permissions department.

All rights reserved, including the right of reproduction in whole or in part, in any form or by any means, electronic or mechanical, including photocopying, recording, or by any information storage and retrieval system, without permission in writing from the Publisher.

Copyright © 2024 by
National Learning Corporation

212 Michael Drive, Syosset, NY 11791
(516) 921-8888 • www.passbooks.com
E-mail: info@passbooks.com

PUBLISHED IN THE UNITED STATES OF AMERICA

PASSBOOK® SERIES

THE *PASSBOOK® SERIES* has been created to prepare applicants and candidates for the ultimate academic battlefield – the examination room.

At some time in our lives, each and every one of us may be required to take an examination – for validation, matriculation, admission, qualification, registration, certification, or licensure.

Based on the assumption that every applicant or candidate has met the basic formal educational standards, has taken the required number of courses, and read the necessary texts, the *PASSBOOK® SERIES* furnishes the one special preparation which may assure passing with confidence, instead of failing with insecurity. Examination questions – together with answers – are furnished as the basic vehicle for study so that the mysteries of the examination and its compounding difficulties may be eliminated or diminished by a sure method.

This book is meant to help you pass your examination provided that you qualify and are serious in your objective.

The entire field is reviewed through the huge store of content information which is succinctly presented through a provocative and challenging approach – the question-and-answer method.

A climate of success is established by furnishing the correct answers at the end of each test.

You soon learn to recognize types of questions, forms of questions, and patterns of questioning. You may even begin to anticipate expected outcomes.

You perceive that many questions are repeated or adapted so that you can gain acute insights, which may enable you to score many sure points.

You learn how to confront new questions, or types of questions, and to attack them confidently and work out the correct answers.

You note objectives and emphases, and recognize pitfalls and dangers, so that you may make positive educational adjustments.

Moreover, you are kept fully informed in relation to new concepts, methods, practices, and directions in the field.

You discover that you are actually taking the examination all the time: you are preparing for the examination by "taking" an examination, not by reading extraneous and/or supererogatory textbooks.

In short, this PASSBOOK®, used directedly, should be an important factor in helping you to pass your test.

COMMUNICATION ELECTRICIAN

DUTIES
A Communication Electrician does skilled work in the maintenance, repair and installation of communication systems and equipment such as microwave, fiber-optic systems, SCADA, data network systems, radio communications transmitters and receivers, telephone, microprocessors, telemetering, subcarrier, and multiplexing; performs related work.

EXAMPLES OF TYPICAL TASKS
Under supervision, Communication Electricians install, maintain and repair the copper and fiber cable and line network, overhead and underground, in connection with fire alarm and communication systems. They locate, clear and repair troubles in the electrical cable and fiber-optic cable and line network; replace and/or extend the cable or aerial line plant including excavating and replacing concrete as necessary; install and replace damaged fire alarm posts and poles including excavating and replacing concrete and asphalt as necessary; maintain and replace electro-mechanical fire alarm boxes, citizen's emergency response boxes and their allied circuits; splice, wipe, solder and terminate lead and/or plastic sheathed cables; install and replace damaged conduit; snake and install cables in conduit in streets, on poles, structures and buildings including excavating and replacing concrete as necessary; operate compressor, pneumatic, hydraulic and power equipment as required in the work; keep records and make reports; may direct the work of assigned subordinate personnel; perform the above tasks in manholes, firehouses, public schools, on poles, bridges, tunnels, expressways, highways, etc., and wherever the electrical cable and fiber-optic cable or aerial plant and its allied equipment exist; operate motor vehicles in carrying out duties and responsibilities; may assume the duties and responsibilities of the supervisor in the temporary absence of that individual; and perform related work.

SCOPE OF THE EXAMINATION
The multiple-choice written test may include questions on testing cables and aerial lines using standard electrical testing apparatus; safe working practices; methods and procedures for the installation, alteration and maintenance of cables and aerial lines; splicing, wiping, soldering and terminating cables; preparing reports and maintaining records; and other related areas.

HOW TO TAKE A TEST

I. YOU MUST PASS AN EXAMINATION

A. WHAT EVERY CANDIDATE SHOULD KNOW

Examination applicants often ask us for help in preparing for the written test. What can I study in advance? What kinds of questions will be asked? How will the test be given? How will the papers be graded?

As an applicant for a civil service examination, you may be wondering about some of these things. Our purpose here is to suggest effective methods of advance study and to describe civil service examinations.

Your chances for success on this examination can be increased if you know how to prepare. Those "pre-examination jitters" can be reduced if you know what to expect. You can even experience an adventure in good citizenship if you know why civil service exams are given.

B. WHY ARE CIVIL SERVICE EXAMINATIONS GIVEN?

Civil service examinations are important to you in two ways. As a citizen, you want public jobs filled by employees who know how to do their work. As a job seeker, you want a fair chance to compete for that job on an equal footing with other candidates. The best-known means of accomplishing this two-fold goal is the competitive examination.

Exams are widely publicized throughout the nation. They may be administered for jobs in federal, state, city, municipal, town or village governments or agencies.

Any citizen may apply, with some limitations, such as the age or residence of applicants. Your experience and education may be reviewed to see whether you meet the requirements for the particular examination. When these requirements exist, they are reasonable and applied consistently to all applicants. Thus, a competitive examination may cause you some uneasiness now, but it is your privilege and safeguard.

C. HOW ARE CIVIL SERVICE EXAMS DEVELOPED?

Examinations are carefully written by trained technicians who are specialists in the field known as "psychological measurement," in consultation with recognized authorities in the field of work that the test will cover. These experts recommend the subject matter areas or skills to be tested; only those knowledges or skills important to your success on the job are included. The most reliable books and source materials available are used as references. Together, the experts and technicians judge the difficulty level of the questions.

Test technicians know how to phrase questions so that the problem is clearly stated. Their ethics do not permit "trick" or "catch" questions. Questions may have been tried out on sample groups, or subjected to statistical analysis, to determine their usefulness.

Written tests are often used in combination with performance tests, ratings of training and experience, and oral interviews. All of these measures combine to form the best-known means of finding the right person for the right job.

II. HOW TO PASS THE WRITTEN TEST

A. NATURE OF THE EXAMINATION

To prepare intelligently for civil service examinations, you should know how they differ from school examinations you have taken. In school you were assigned certain definite pages to read or subjects to cover. The examination questions were quite detailed and usually emphasized memory. Civil service exams, on the other hand, try to discover your present ability to perform the duties of a position, plus your potentiality to learn these duties. In other words, a civil service exam attempts to predict how successful you will be. Questions cover such a broad area that they cannot be as minute and detailed as school exam questions.

In the public service similar kinds of work, or positions, are grouped together in one "class." This process is known as *position-classification*. All the positions in a class are paid according to the salary range for that class. One class title covers all of these positions, and they are all tested by the same examination.

B. FOUR BASIC STEPS

1) Study the announcement

How, then, can you know what subjects to study? Our best answer is: "Learn as much as possible about the class of positions for which you've applied." The exam will test the knowledge, skills and abilities needed to do the work.

Your most valuable source of information about the position you want is the official exam announcement. This announcement lists the training and experience qualifications. Check these standards and apply only if you come reasonably close to meeting them.

The brief description of the position in the examination announcement offers some clues to the subjects which will be tested. Think about the job itself. Review the duties in your mind. Can you perform them, or are there some in which you are rusty? Fill in the blank spots in your preparation.

Many jurisdictions preview the written test in the exam announcement by including a section called "Knowledge and Abilities Required," "Scope of the Examination," or some similar heading. Here you will find out specifically what fields will be tested.

2) Review your own background

Once you learn in general what the position is all about, and what you need to know to do the work, ask yourself which subjects you already know fairly well and which need improvement. You may wonder whether to concentrate on improving your strong areas or on building some background in your fields of weakness. When the announcement has specified "some knowledge" or "considerable knowledge," or has used adjectives like "beginning principles of…" or "advanced … methods," you can get a clue as to the number and difficulty of questions to be asked in any given field. More questions, and hence broader coverage, would be included for those subjects which are more important in the work. Now weigh your strengths and weaknesses against the job requirements and prepare accordingly.

3) Determine the level of the position

Another way to tell how intensively you should prepare is to understand the level of the job for which you are applying. Is it the entering level? In other words, is this the position in which beginners in a field of work are hired? Or is it an intermediate or advanced level? Sometimes this is indicated by such words as "Junior" or "Senior" in the class title. Other jurisdictions use Roman numerals to designate the level – Clerk I, Clerk II, for example. The word "Supervisor" sometimes appears in the title. If the level is not indicated by the title, check the description of duties. Will you be working under very close supervision, or will you have responsibility for independent decisions in this work?

4) Choose appropriate study materials

Now that you know the subjects to be examined and the relative amount of each subject to be covered, you can choose suitable study materials. For beginning level jobs, or even advanced ones, if you have a pronounced weakness in some aspect of your training, read a modern, standard textbook in that field. Be sure it is up to date and has general coverage. Such books are normally available at your library, and the librarian will be glad to help you locate one. For entry-level positions, questions of appropriate difficulty are chosen -- neither highly advanced questions, nor those too simple. Such questions require careful thought but not advanced training.

If the position for which you are applying is technical or advanced, you will read more advanced, specialized material. If you are already familiar with the basic principles of your field, elementary textbooks would waste your time. Concentrate on advanced textbooks and technical periodicals. Think through the concepts and review difficult problems in your field.

These are all general sources. You can get more ideas on your own initiative, following these leads. For example, training manuals and publications of the government agency which employs workers in your field can be useful, particularly for technical and professional positions. A letter or visit to the government department involved may result in more specific study suggestions, and certainly will provide you with a more definite idea of the exact nature of the position you are seeking.

III. KINDS OF TESTS

Tests are used for purposes other than measuring knowledge and ability to perform specified duties. For some positions, it is equally important to test ability to make adjustments to new situations or to profit from training. In others, basic mental abilities not dependent on information are essential. Questions which test these things may not appear as pertinent to the duties of the position as those which test for knowledge and information. Yet they are often highly important parts of a fair examination. For very general questions, it is almost impossible to help you direct your study efforts. What we can do is to point out some of the more common of these general abilities needed in public service positions and describe some typical questions.

1) General information

Broad, general information has been found useful for predicting job success in some kinds of work. This is tested in a variety of ways, from vocabulary lists to questions about current events. Basic background in some field of work, such as sociology or economics, may be sampled in a group of questions. Often these are principles which have become familiar to most persons through exposure rather than through formal training. It is difficult to advise you how to study for these questions; being alert to the world around you is our best suggestion.

2) Verbal ability

An example of an ability needed in many positions is verbal or language ability. Verbal ability is, in brief, the ability to use and understand words. Vocabulary and grammar tests are typical measures of this ability. Reading comprehension or paragraph interpretation questions are common in many kinds of civil service tests. You are given a paragraph of written material and asked to find its central meaning.

3) Numerical ability

Number skills can be tested by the familiar arithmetic problem, by checking paired lists of numbers to see which are alike and which are different, or by interpreting charts and graphs. In the latter test, a graph may be printed in the test booklet which you are asked to use as the basis for answering questions.

4) Observation

A popular test for law-enforcement positions is the observation test. A picture is shown to you for several minutes, then taken away. Questions about the picture test your ability to observe both details and larger elements.

5) Following directions

In many positions in the public service, the employee must be able to carry out written instructions dependably and accurately. You may be given a chart with several columns, each column listing a variety of information. The questions require you to carry out directions involving the information given in the chart.

6) Skills and aptitudes

Performance tests effectively measure some manual skills and aptitudes. When the skill is one in which you are trained, such as typing or shorthand, you can practice. These tests are often very much like those given in business school or high school courses. For many of the other skills and aptitudes, however, no short-time preparation can be made. Skills and abilities natural to you or that you have developed throughout your lifetime are being tested.

Many of the general questions just described provide all the data needed to answer the questions and ask you to use your reasoning ability to find the answers. Your best preparation for these tests, as well as for tests of facts and ideas, is to be at your physical and mental best. You, no doubt, have your own methods of getting into an exam-taking mood and keeping "in shape." The next section lists some ideas on this subject.

IV. KINDS OF QUESTIONS

Only rarely is the "essay" question, which you answer in narrative form, used in civil service tests. Civil service tests are usually of the short-answer type. Full instructions for answering these questions will be given to you at the examination. But in case this is your first experience with short-answer questions and separate answer sheets, here is what you need to know:

1) Multiple-choice Questions

Most popular of the short-answer questions is the "multiple choice" or "best answer" question. It can be used, for example, to test for factual knowledge, ability to solve problems or judgment in meeting situations found at work.

A multiple-choice question is normally one of three types—
- It can begin with an incomplete statement followed by several possible endings. You are to find the one ending which *best* completes the statement, although some of the others may not be entirely wrong.
- It can also be a complete statement in the form of a question which is answered by choosing one of the statements listed.

- It can be in the form of a problem – again you select the best answer.

Here is an example of a multiple-choice question with a discussion which should give you some clues as to the method for choosing the right answer:

When an employee has a complaint about his assignment, the action which will *best* help him overcome his difficulty is to
   A. discuss his difficulty with his coworkers
   B. take the problem to the head of the organization
   C. take the problem to the person who gave him the assignment
   D. say nothing to anyone about his complaint

In answering this question, you should study each of the choices to find which is best. Consider choice "A" – Certainly an employee may discuss his complaint with fellow employees, but no change or improvement can result, and the complaint remains unresolved. Choice "B" is a poor choice since the head of the organization probably does not know what assignment you have been given, and taking your problem to him is known as "going over the head" of the supervisor. The supervisor, or person who made the assignment, is the person who can clarify it or correct any injustice. Choice "C" is, therefore, correct. To say nothing, as in choice "D," is unwise. Supervisors have and interest in knowing the problems employees are facing, and the employee is seeking a solution to his problem.

2) True/False Questions

The "true/false" or "right/wrong" form of question is sometimes used. Here a complete statement is given. Your job is to decide whether the statement is right or wrong.

SAMPLE: A roaming cell-phone call to a nearby city costs less than a non-roaming call to a distant city.

This statement is wrong, or false, since roaming calls are more expensive.
This is not a complete list of all possible question forms, although most of the others are variations of these common types. You will always get complete directions for answering questions. Be sure you understand *how* to mark your answers – ask questions until you do.

V. RECORDING YOUR ANSWERS

Computer terminals are used more and more today for many different kinds of exams.
For an examination with very few applicants, you may be told to record your answers in the test booklet itself. Separate answer sheets are much more common. If this separate answer sheet is to be scored by machine – and this is often the case – it is highly important that you mark your answers correctly in order to get credit.
An electronic scoring machine is often used in civil service offices because of the speed with which papers can be scored. Machine-scored answer sheets must be marked with a pencil, which will be given to you. This pencil has a high graphite content which responds to the electronic scoring machine. As a matter of fact, stray dots may register as answers, so do not let your pencil rest on the answer sheet while you are pondering the correct answer. Also, if your pencil lead breaks or is otherwise defective, ask for another.

Since the answer sheet will be dropped in a slot in the scoring machine, be careful not to bend the corners or get the paper crumpled.

The answer sheet normally has five vertical columns of numbers, with 30 numbers to a column. These numbers correspond to the question numbers in your test booklet. After each number, going across the page are four or five pairs of dotted lines. These short dotted lines have small letters or numbers above them. The first two pairs may also have a "T" or "F" above the letters. This indicates that the first two pairs only are to be used if the questions are of the true-false type. If the questions are multiple choice, disregard the "T" and "F" and pay attention only to the small letters or numbers.

Answer your questions in the manner of the sample that follows:

32. The largest city in the United States is
    A. Washington, D.C.
    B. New York City
    C. Chicago
    D. Detroit
    E. San Francisco

1) Choose the answer you think is best. (New York City is the largest, so "B" is correct.)
2) Find the row of dotted lines numbered the same as the question you are answering. (Find row number 32)
3) Find the pair of dotted lines corresponding to the answer. (Find the pair of lines under the mark "B.")
4) Make a solid black mark between the dotted lines.

VI. BEFORE THE TEST

Common sense will help you find procedures to follow to get ready for an examination. Too many of us, however, overlook these sensible measures. Indeed, nervousness and fatigue have been found to be the most serious reasons why applicants fail to do their best on civil service tests. Here is a list of reminders:

- Begin your preparation early – Don't wait until the last minute to go scurrying around for books and materials or to find out what the position is all about.
- Prepare continuously – An hour a night for a week is better than an all-night cram session. This has been definitely established. What is more, a night a week for a month will return better dividends than crowding your study into a shorter period of time.
- Locate the place of the exam – You have been sent a notice telling you when and where to report for the examination. If the location is in a different town or otherwise unfamiliar to you, it would be well to inquire the best route and learn something about the building.
- Relax the night before the test – Allow your mind to rest. Do not study at all that night. Plan some mild recreation or diversion; then go to bed early and get a good night's sleep.
- Get up early enough to make a leisurely trip to the place for the test – This way unforeseen events, traffic snarls, unfamiliar buildings, etc. will not upset you.
- Dress comfortably – A written test is not a fashion show. You will be known by number and not by name, so wear something comfortable.

- Leave excess paraphernalia at home – Shopping bags and odd bundles will get in your way. You need bring only the items mentioned in the official notice you received; usually everything you need is provided. Do not bring reference books to the exam. They will only confuse those last minutes and be taken away from you when in the test room.
- Arrive somewhat ahead of time – If because of transportation schedules you must get there very early, bring a newspaper or magazine to take your mind off yourself while waiting.
- Locate the examination room – When you have found the proper room, you will be directed to the seat or part of the room where you will sit. Sometimes you are given a sheet of instructions to read while you are waiting. Do not fill out any forms until you are told to do so; just read them and be prepared.
- Relax and prepare to listen to the instructions
- If you have any physical problem that may keep you from doing your best, be sure to tell the test administrator. If you are sick or in poor health, you really cannot do your best on the exam. You can come back and take the test some other time.

VII. AT THE TEST

The day of the test is here and you have the test booklet in your hand. The temptation to get going is very strong. Caution! There is more to success than knowing the right answers. You must know how to identify your papers and understand variations in the type of short-answer question used in this particular examination. Follow these suggestions for maximum results from your efforts:

1) Cooperate with the monitor

The test administrator has a duty to create a situation in which you can be as much at ease as possible. He will give instructions, tell you when to begin, check to see that you are marking your answer sheet correctly, and so on. He is not there to guard you, although he will see that your competitors do not take unfair advantage. He wants to help you do your best.

2) Listen to all instructions

Don't jump the gun! Wait until you understand all directions. In most civil service tests you get more time than you need to answer the questions. So don't be in a hurry. Read each word of instructions until you clearly understand the meaning. Study the examples, listen to all announcements and follow directions. Ask questions if you do not understand what to do.

3) Identify your papers

Civil service exams are usually identified by number only. You will be assigned a number; you must not put your name on your test papers. Be sure to copy your number correctly. Since more than one exam may be given, copy your exact examination title.

4) Plan your time

Unless you are told that a test is a "speed" or "rate of work" test, speed itself is usually not important. Time enough to answer all the questions will be provided, but this does not mean that you have all day. An overall time limit has been set. Divide the total time (in minutes) by the number of questions to determine the approximate time you have for each question.

5) Do not linger over difficult questions

If you come across a difficult question, mark it with a paper clip (useful to have along) and come back to it when you have been through the booklet. One caution if you do this – be sure to skip a number on your answer sheet as well. Check often to be sure that you have not lost your place and that you are marking in the row numbered the same as the question you are answering.

6) Read the questions

Be sure you know what the question asks! Many capable people are unsuccessful because they failed to *read* the questions correctly.

7) Answer all questions

Unless you have been instructed that a penalty will be deducted for incorrect answers, it is better to guess than to omit a question.

8) Speed tests

It is often better NOT to guess on speed tests. It has been found that on timed tests people are tempted to spend the last few seconds before time is called in marking answers at random – without even reading them – in the hope of picking up a few extra points. To discourage this practice, the instructions may warn you that your score will be "corrected" for guessing. That is, a penalty will be applied. The incorrect answers will be deducted from the correct ones, or some other penalty formula will be used.

9) Review your answers

If you finish before time is called, go back to the questions you guessed or omitted to give them further thought. Review other answers if you have time.

10) Return your test materials

If you are ready to leave before others have finished or time is called, take ALL your materials to the monitor and leave quietly. Never take any test material with you. The monitor can discover whose papers are not complete, and taking a test booklet may be grounds for disqualification.

VIII. EXAMINATION TECHNIQUES

1) Read the general instructions carefully. These are usually printed on the first page of the exam booklet. As a rule, these instructions refer to the timing of the examination; the fact that you should not start work until the signal and must stop work at a signal, etc. If there are any *special* instructions, such as a choice of questions to be answered, make sure that you note this instruction carefully.

2) When you are ready to start work on the examination, that is as soon as the signal has been given, read the instructions to each question booklet, underline any key words or phrases, such as *least, best, outline, describe* and the like. In this way you will tend to answer as requested rather than discover on reviewing your paper that you *listed without describing*, that you selected the *worst* choice rather than the *best* choice, etc.

3) If the examination is of the objective or multiple-choice type – that is, each question will also give a series of possible answers: A, B, C or D, and you are called upon to select the best answer and write the letter next to that answer on your answer paper – it is advisable to start answering each question in turn. There may be anywhere from 50 to 100 such questions in the three or four hours allotted and you can see how much time would be taken if you read through all the questions before beginning to answer any. Furthermore, if you come across a question or group of questions which you know would be difficult to answer, it would undoubtedly affect your handling of all the other questions.

4) If the examination is of the essay type and contains but a few questions, it is a moot point as to whether you should read all the questions before starting to answer any one. Of course, if you are given a choice – say five out of seven and the like – then it is essential to read all the questions so you can eliminate the two that are most difficult. If, however, you are asked to answer all the questions, there may be danger in trying to answer the easiest one first because you may find that you will spend too much time on it. The best technique is to answer the first question, then proceed to the second, etc.

5) Time your answers. Before the exam begins, write down the time it started, then add the time allowed for the examination and write down the time it must be completed, then divide the time available somewhat as follows:
   - If 3-1/2 hours are allowed, that would be 210 minutes. If you have 80 objective-type questions, that would be an average of 2-1/2 minutes per question. Allow yourself no more than 2 minutes per question, or a total of 160 minutes, which will permit about 50 minutes to review.
   - If for the time allotment of 210 minutes there are 7 essay questions to answer, that would average about 30 minutes a question. Give yourself only 25 minutes per question so that you have about 35 minutes to review.

6) The most important instruction is to *read each question* and make sure you know what is wanted. The second most important instruction is to *time yourself properly* so that you answer every question. The third most important instruction is to *answer every question*. Guess if you have to but include something for each question. Remember that you will receive no credit for a blank and will probably receive some credit if you write something in answer to an essay question. If you guess a letter – say "B" for a multiple-choice question – you may have guessed right. If you leave a blank as an answer to a multiple-choice question, the examiners may respect your feelings but it will not add a point to your score. Some exams may penalize you for wrong answers, so in such cases *only*, you may not want to guess unless you have some basis for your answer.

7) Suggestions
   a. Objective-type questions
      1. Examine the question booklet for proper sequence of pages and questions
      2. Read all instructions carefully
      3. Skip any question which seems too difficult; return to it after all other questions have been answered
      4. Apportion your time properly; do not spend too much time on any single question or group of questions

5. Note and underline key words – *all, most, fewest, least, best, worst, same, opposite,* etc.
6. Pay particular attention to negatives
7. Note unusual option, e.g., unduly long, short, complex, different or similar in content to the body of the question
8. Observe the use of "hedging" words – *probably, may, most likely,* etc.
9. Make sure that your answer is put next to the same number as the question
10. Do not second-guess unless you have good reason to believe the second answer is definitely more correct
11. Cross out original answer if you decide another answer is more accurate; do not erase until you are ready to hand your paper in
12. Answer all questions; guess unless instructed otherwise
13. Leave time for review

b. Essay questions
1. Read each question carefully
2. Determine exactly what is wanted. Underline key words or phrases.
3. Decide on outline or paragraph answer
4. Include many different points and elements unless asked to develop any one or two points or elements
5. Show impartiality by giving pros and cons unless directed to select one side only
6. Make and write down any assumptions you find necessary to answer the questions
7. Watch your English, grammar, punctuation and choice of words
8. Time your answers; don't crowd material

8) Answering the essay question

Most essay questions can be answered by framing the specific response around several key words or ideas. Here are a few such key words or ideas:

M's: manpower, materials, methods, money, management
P's: purpose, program, policy, plan, procedure, practice, problems, pitfalls, personnel, public relations

a. Six basic steps in handling problems:
1. Preliminary plan and background development
2. Collect information, data and facts
3. Analyze and interpret information, data and facts
4. Analyze and develop solutions as well as make recommendations
5. Prepare report and sell recommendations
6. Install recommendations and follow up effectiveness

b. Pitfalls to avoid
1. *Taking things for granted* – A statement of the situation does not necessarily imply that each of the elements is necessarily true; for example, a complaint may be invalid and biased so that all that can be taken for granted is that a complaint has been registered

2. *Considering only one side of a situation* – Wherever possible, indicate several alternatives and then point out the reasons you selected the best one
3. *Failing to indicate follow up* – Whenever your answer indicates action on your part, make certain that you will take proper follow-up action to see how successful your recommendations, procedures or actions turn out to be
4. *Taking too long in answering any single question* – Remember to time your answers properly

IX. AFTER THE TEST

Scoring procedures differ in detail among civil service jurisdictions although the general principles are the same. Whether the papers are hand-scored or graded by machine we have described, they are nearly always graded by number. That is, the person who marks the paper knows only the number – never the name – of the applicant. Not until all the papers have been graded will they be matched with names. If other tests, such as training and experience or oral interview ratings have been given, scores will be combined. Different parts of the examination usually have different weights. For example, the written test might count 60 percent of the final grade, and a rating of training and experience 40 percent. In many jurisdictions, veterans will have a certain number of points added to their grades.

After the final grade has been determined, the names are placed in grade order and an eligible list is established. There are various methods for resolving ties between those who get the same final grade – probably the most common is to place first the name of the person whose application was received first. Job offers are made from the eligible list in the order the names appear on it. You will be notified of your grade and your rank as soon as all these computations have been made. This will be done as rapidly as possible.

People who are found to meet the requirements in the announcement are called "eligibles." Their names are put on a list of eligible candidates. An eligible's chances of getting a job depend on how high he stands on this list and how fast agencies are filling jobs from the list.

When a job is to be filled from a list of eligibles, the agency asks for the names of people on the list of eligibles for that job. When the civil service commission receives this request, it sends to the agency the names of the three people highest on this list. Or, if the job to be filled has specialized requirements, the office sends the agency the names of the top three persons who meet these requirements from the general list.

The appointing officer makes a choice from among the three people whose names were sent to him. If the selected person accepts the appointment, the names of the others are put back on the list to be considered for future openings.

That is the rule in hiring from all kinds of eligible lists, whether they are for typist, carpenter, chemist, or something else. For every vacancy, the appointing officer has his choice of any one of the top three eligibles on the list. This explains why the person whose name is on top of the list sometimes does not get an appointment when some of the persons lower on the list do. If the appointing officer chooses the second or third eligible, the No. 1 eligible does not get a job at once, but stays on the list until he is appointed or the list is terminated.

X. HOW TO PASS THE INTERVIEW TEST

The examination for which you applied requires an oral interview test. You have already taken the written test and you are now being called for the interview test – the final part of the formal examination.

You may think that it is not possible to prepare for an interview test and that there are no procedures to follow during an interview. Our purpose is to point out some things you can do in advance that will help you and some good rules to follow and pitfalls to avoid while you are being interviewed.

What is an interview supposed to test?

The written examination is designed to test the technical knowledge and competence of the candidate; the oral is designed to evaluate intangible qualities, not readily measured otherwise, and to establish a list showing the relative fitness of each candidate – as measured against his competitors – for the position sought. Scoring is not on the basis of "right" and "wrong," but on a sliding scale of values ranging from "not passable" to "outstanding." As a matter of fact, it is possible to achieve a relatively low score without a single "incorrect" answer because of evident weakness in the qualities being measured.

Occasionally, an examination may consist entirely of an oral test – either an individual or a group oral. In such cases, information is sought concerning the technical knowledges and abilities of the candidate, since there has been no written examination for this purpose. More commonly, however, an oral test is used to supplement a written examination.

Who conducts interviews?

The composition of oral boards varies among different jurisdictions. In nearly all, a representative of the personnel department serves as chairman. One of the members of the board may be a representative of the department in which the candidate would work. In some cases, "outside experts" are used, and, frequently, a businessman or some other representative of the general public is asked to serve. Labor and management or other special groups may be represented. The aim is to secure the services of experts in the appropriate field.

However the board is composed, it is a good idea (and not at all improper or unethical) to ascertain in advance of the interview who the members are and what groups they represent. When you are introduced to them, you will have some idea of their backgrounds and interests, and at least you will not stutter and stammer over their names.

What should be done before the interview?

While knowledge about the board members is useful and takes some of the surprise element out of the interview, there is other preparation which is more substantive. It *is* possible to prepare for an oral interview – in several ways:

1) Keep a copy of your application and review it carefully before the interview

This may be the only document before the oral board, and the starting point of the interview. Know what education and experience you have listed there, and the sequence and dates of all of it. Sometimes the board will ask you to review the highlights of your experience for them; you should not have to hem and haw doing it.

2) Study the class specification and the examination announcement

Usually, the oral board has one or both of these to guide them. The qualities, characteristics or knowledges required by the position sought are stated in these documents. They offer valuable clues as to the nature of the oral interview. For example, if the job involves supervisory responsibilities, the announcement will usually indicate that knowledge of modern supervisory methods and the qualifications of the candidate as a supervisor will be tested. If so, you can expect such questions, frequently in the form of a hypothetical situation which you are expected to solve. NEVER go into an oral without knowledge of the duties and responsibilities of the job you seek.

3) Think through each qualification required
Try to visualize the kind of questions you would ask if you were a board member. How well could you answer them? Try especially to appraise your own knowledge and background in each area, *measured against the job sought*, and identify any areas in which you are weak. Be critical and realistic – do not flatter yourself.

4) Do some general reading in areas in which you feel you may be weak
For example, if the job involves supervision and your past experience has NOT, some general reading in supervisory methods and practices, particularly in the field of human relations, might be useful. Do NOT study agency procedures or detailed manuals. The oral board will be testing your understanding and capacity, not your memory.

5) Get a good night's sleep and watch your general health and mental attitude
You will want a clear head at the interview. Take care of a cold or any other minor ailment, and of course, no hangovers.

What should be done on the day of the interview?
Now comes the day of the interview itself. Give yourself plenty of time to get there. Plan to arrive somewhat ahead of the scheduled time, particularly if your appointment is in the fore part of the day. If a previous candidate fails to appear, the board might be ready for you a bit early. By early afternoon an oral board is almost invariably behind schedule if there are many candidates, and you may have to wait. Take along a book or magazine to read, or your application to review, but leave any extraneous material in the waiting room when you go in for your interview. In any event, relax and compose yourself.

The matter of dress is important. The board is forming impressions about you – from your experience, your manners, your attitude, and your appearance. Give your personal appearance careful attention. Dress your best, but not your flashiest. Choose conservative, appropriate clothing, and be sure it is immaculate. This is a business interview, and your appearance should indicate that you regard it as such. Besides, being well groomed and properly dressed will help boost your confidence.

Sooner or later, someone will call your name and escort you into the interview room. *This is it*. From here on you are on your own. It is too late for any more preparation. But remember, you asked for this opportunity to prove your fitness, and you are here because your request was granted.

What happens when you go in?
The usual sequence of events will be as follows: The clerk (who is often the board stenographer) will introduce you to the chairman of the oral board, who will introduce you to the other members of the board. Acknowledge the introductions before you sit down. Do not be surprised if you find a microphone facing you or a stenotypist sitting by. Oral interviews are usually recorded in the event of an appeal or other review.

Usually the chairman of the board will open the interview by reviewing the highlights of your education and work experience from your application – primarily for the benefit of the other members of the board, as well as to get the material into the record. Do not interrupt or comment unless there is an error or significant misinterpretation; if that is the case, do not hesitate. But do not quibble about insignificant matters. Also, he will usually ask you some question about your education, experience or your present job – partly to get you to start talking and to establish the interviewing "rapport." He may start the actual questioning, or turn it over to one of the other members. Frequently, each member undertakes the questioning on a particular area, one in which he is perhaps most competent, so you can expect each member to participate in the examination. Because time is limited, you may also expect some rather abrupt switches in the direction the questioning takes, so do not be upset by it. Normally, a board member will not pursue a single line of questioning unless he discovers a particular strength or weakness.

After each member has participated, the chairman will usually ask whether any member has any further questions, then will ask you if you have anything you wish to add. Unless you are expecting this question, it may floor you. Worse, it may start you off on an extended, extemporaneous speech. The board is not usually seeking more information. The question is principally to offer you a last opportunity to present further qualifications or to indicate that you have nothing to add. So, if you feel that a significant qualification or characteristic has been overlooked, it is proper to point it out in a sentence or so. Do not compliment the board on the thoroughness of their examination – they have been sketchy, and you know it. If you wish, merely say, "No thank you, I have nothing further to add." This is a point where you can "talk yourself out" of a good impression or fail to present an important bit of information. Remember, *you close the interview yourself.*

The chairman will then say, "That is all, Mr. _____, thank you." Do not be startled; the interview is over, and quicker than you think. Thank him, gather your belongings and take your leave. Save your sigh of relief for the other side of the door.

How to put your best foot forward

Throughout this entire process, you may feel that the board individually and collectively is trying to pierce your defenses, seek out your hidden weaknesses and embarrass and confuse you. Actually, this is not true. They are obliged to make an appraisal of your qualifications for the job you are seeking, and they want to see you in your best light. Remember, they must interview all candidates and a non-cooperative candidate may become a failure in spite of their best efforts to bring out his qualifications. Here are 15 suggestions that will help you:

1) **Be natural – Keep your attitude confident, not cocky**

If you are not confident that you can do the job, do not expect the board to be. Do not apologize for your weaknesses, try to bring out your strong points. The board is interested in a positive, not negative, presentation. Cockiness will antagonize any board member and make him wonder if you are covering up a weakness by a false show of strength.

2) **Get comfortable, but don't lounge or sprawl**

Sit erectly but not stiffly. A careless posture may lead the board to conclude that you are careless in other things, or at least that you are not impressed by the importance of the occasion. Either conclusion is natural, even if incorrect. Do not fuss with your clothing, a pencil or an ashtray. Your hands may occasionally be useful to emphasize a point; do not let them become a point of distraction.

3) **Do not wisecrack or make small talk**

This is a serious situation, and your attitude should show that you consider it as such. Further, the time of the board is limited – they do not want to waste it, and neither should you.

4) Do not exaggerate your experience or abilities

In the first place, from information in the application or other interviews and sources, the board may know more about you than you think. Secondly, you probably will not get away with it. An experienced board is rather adept at spotting such a situation, so do not take the chance.

5) If you know a board member, do not make a point of it, yet do not hide it

Certainly you are not fooling him, and probably not the other members of the board. Do not try to take advantage of your acquaintanceship – it will probably do you little good.

6) Do not dominate the interview

Let the board do that. They will give you the clues – do not assume that you have to do all the talking. Realize that the board has a number of questions to ask you, and do not try to take up all the interview time by showing off your extensive knowledge of the answer to the first one.

7) Be attentive

You only have 20 minutes or so, and you should keep your attention at its sharpest throughout. When a member is addressing a problem or question to you, give him your undivided attention. Address your reply principally to him, but do not exclude the other board members.

8) Do not interrupt

A board member may be stating a problem for you to analyze. He will ask you a question when the time comes. Let him state the problem, and wait for the question.

9) Make sure you understand the question

Do not try to answer until you are sure what the question is. If it is not clear, restate it in your own words or ask the board member to clarify it for you. However, do not haggle about minor elements.

10) Reply promptly but not hastily

A common entry on oral board rating sheets is "candidate responded readily," or "candidate hesitated in replies." Respond as promptly and quickly as you can, but do not jump to a hasty, ill-considered answer.

11) Do not be peremptory in your answers

A brief answer is proper – but do not fire your answer back. That is a losing game from your point of view. The board member can probably ask questions much faster than you can answer them.

12) Do not try to create the answer you think the board member wants

He is interested in what kind of mind you have and how it works – not in playing games. Furthermore, he can usually spot this practice and will actually grade you down on it.

13) Do not switch sides in your reply merely to agree with a board member

Frequently, a member will take a contrary position merely to draw you out and to see if you are willing and able to defend your point of view. Do not start a debate, yet do not surrender a good position. If a position is worth taking, it is worth defending.

14) Do not be afraid to admit an error in judgment if you are shown to be wrong

The board knows that you are forced to reply without any opportunity for careful consideration. Your answer may be demonstrably wrong. If so, admit it and get on with the interview.

15) Do not dwell at length on your present job

The opening question may relate to your present assignment. Answer the question but do not go into an extended discussion. You are being examined for a *new* job, not your present one. As a matter of fact, try to phrase ALL your answers in terms of the job for which you are being examined.

Basis of Rating

Probably you will forget most of these "do's" and "don'ts" when you walk into the oral interview room. Even remembering them all will not ensure you a passing grade. Perhaps you did not have the qualifications in the first place. But remembering them will help you to put your best foot forward, without treading on the toes of the board members.

Rumor and popular opinion to the contrary notwithstanding, an oral board wants you to make the best appearance possible. They know you are under pressure – but they also want to see how you respond to it as a guide to what your reaction would be under the pressures of the job you seek. They will be influenced by the degree of poise you display, the personal traits you show and the manner in which you respond.

ABOUT THIS BOOK

This book contains tests divided into Examination Sections. Go through each test, answering every question in the margin. We have also attached a sample answer sheet at the back of the book that can be removed and used. At the end of each test look at the answer key and check your answers. On the ones you got wrong, look at the right answer choice and learn. Do not fill in the answers first. Do not memorize the questions and answers, but understand the answer and principles involved. On your test, the questions will likely be different from the samples. Questions are changed and new ones added. If you understand these past questions you should have success with any changes that arise. Tests may consist of several types of questions. We have additional books on each subject should more study be advisable or necessary for you. Finally, the more you study, the better prepared you will be. This book is intended to be the last thing you study before you walk into the examination room. Prior study of relevant texts is also recommended. NLC publishes some of these in our Fundamental Series. Knowledge and good sense are important factors in passing your exam. Good luck also helps. So now study this Passbook, absorb the material contained within and take that knowledge into the examination. Then do your best to pass that exam.

EXAMINATION SECTION

EXAMINATION SECTION
TEST 1

DIRECTIONS: Each question or incomplete statement is followed by several suggested answers or completions. Select the one that BEST answers the question or completes the statement. *PRINT THE LETTER OF THE CORRECT ANSWER IN THE SPACE AT THE RIGHT.*

1. Circular waveguides are preferred to rectangular ones for some applications because of   1.____

    A. freedom from spurious modes
    B. rotation of polarization
    C. lower attenuation
    D. smaller cross section needed at any frequency

2. Tropospheric scatter is used with frequencies in the _____ range.   2.____

    A. VLF   B. HF   C. VHF   D. UHF

3. The method of monitoring telephone call duration for later customer invoicing is known as   3.____

    A. propagation check   B. singing
    C. primary rate timing   D. pulse metering

4. What is the term for the device inserted at an intermediate stage of a digital transmission line to counteract the effects of signal deterioration?   4.____

    A. Regenerator   B. Amplifier
    C. Pulse modulator D. Repeater

5. For transmission-line load matching over a range of frequencies, it is BEST to use a   5.____

    A. single stub of adjustable position
    B. double stub
    C. broadband directional coupler
    D. balun

6. Which type of noise occurs ONLY in data circuits?   6.____

    A. Thermal   B. Impulse
    C. Notched   D. Quantizing

7. Which of the following is a type of detector used in optical fiber systems?   7.____

    A. PIN   B. WAN   C. LED   D. ILD

8. A binary digit of value *1* is known as a(n)   8.____

    A. bit   B. word   C. code   D. mark

9. To reduce quantizing noise,   9.____

    A. *increase* the number of samples per second
    B. *increase* the number of standard amplitudes
    C. use an RF amplifier in the receiver
    D. send pulses whose sides are more nearly vertical

1

10. The _____ type of facsimile recording uses chemically treated paper that is decomposed by an electric current.

    A. electrothermal
    B. electrolytic
    C. electropercussive
    D. electrostatic

11. Which of the following types of line terminal measurements performed on an optical fiber system is a simple periodic check to ensure that the LD is healthy?

    A. BER
    B. Output pulse waveform
    C. Optical output power
    D. Protection switching

12. In coaxial cable systems using the cable type LI, repeaters are nominally spaced _____ mile(s) apart.

    A. 1   B. 2   C. 4   D. 8

13. Which of the following is a possible use for SAW devices?

    A. Filters
    B. Oscillators at millimeter frequencies
    C. UHF amplifiers
    D. Stripline-type transmission media

14. A forward error-correcting code operates in a digital comnunication system by

    A. using parity to correct the errors in all cases
    B. requiring retransmission of the entire signal
    C. requiring partial retransmission of the signal
    D. requiring no part of the signal to be retransmitted

15. Which of the following components of a PCM transmission will be different in 24- and 30-channel systems?

    A. Sampling frequency
    B. Number of bits per code word
    C. Bit transfer rate
    D. Frame period

16. Each of the following reason why a 3-GHz waveguide might be preferred over an equivalent transmission line EXCEPT

    A. it is not as bulky as the transmission lines
    B. it has lower attenuation
    C. it is able to carry higher powers
    D. it suffers less signal loss

17. Which of the following is contained within a submarine cable repeater?

    A. Pilot inject and extract equipment
    B. Multiplexing and demultiplexing equipment
    C. Filters for the two transmission directions
    D. A DC power supply and regulator

18. According to the present North American telephone subscriber loop design rules, a loop using the GREG design parameter must have a loop resistance of

    A. 1300 Ω maximum
    B. 1301-3600 Ω
    C. 1501-2800 Ω
    D. 0-2800 Ω

19. A good blocking performance in an FM receiver

    A. is unaffected by AGC generated by nearby transmissions
    B. does not suffer from double-spotting
    C. suffers from detector burnout
    D. has poor image frequency rejection

20. A signal impairment caused by different speeds of propagation of the component frequencies of a complex signal is termed a

    A. harmonic disturbance
    B. group delay
    C. envelope delay
    D. crosstalk

21. Which type of optical fiber dispersion is due to the frequency dependence of the fiber's refractive index?

    A. Modal
    B. Material
    C. Waveguide
    D. Multimodal

22. Of the following, a _____ is NOT a TWT slow-wave structure.

    A. coupled cavity
    B. helix
    C. ring-bar
    D. periodic-permanent magnet

23. Which of the following types of noise disturbances in a communications circuit consists of irregular noise spikes of relatively high amplitude?

    A. Thermal noise
    B. Intermodulation noise
    C. Impulse noise
    D. Crosstalk

24. A telecommunications device allowing two-way transmission of signals in one direction at a time is called a

    A. group
    B. half duplex
    C. hybrid
    D. duplex

25. High-frequency waves are

    A. capable of use for long-distance communications on the moon
    B. affected by the solar cycle
    C. reflected by the D layer
    D. absorbed by the F2 layer

KEY (CORRECT ANSWERS)

1.	C	11.	C
2.	A	12.	D
3.	D	13.	A
4.	A	14.	D
5.	B	15.	C
6.	C	16.	A
7.	A	17.	C
8.	D	18.	D
9.	B	19.	A
10.	A	20.	B

21. B
22. D
23. C
24. B
25. B

TEST 2

DIRECTIONS: Each question or incomplete statement is followed by several suggested answers or completions. Select the one that BEST answers the question or completes the statement. *PRINT THE LETTER OF THE CORRECT ANSWER IN THE SPACE AT THE RIGHT.*

1. The phenomenon of microwaves following the curvature of the earth is termed 1.____

   A. ducting
   B. hop
   C. troposcatter
   D. the Faraday effect

2. When EM waves are reflected at an angle from a wall, their wavelength along the wall is 2.____

   A. the same as the wavelength perpendicular to the wall
   B. greater than in the actual direction of propagation
   C. shortened by the Doppler effect
   D. the same as in free space

3. Which type of cellular radio system uses a typical carrier bandwidth of 200 kHz? 3.____

   A. Digital FDMA
   B. Digital narrowband TDMA
   C. Analog FM
   D. Digital wideband

4. The gain-bandwidth frequency of a microwave transistor is the frequency at which the 4.____

   A. power gain of the transistor falls to unity
   B. alpha of the transistor falls by 3 dB
   C. beta of the transistor falls to unity
   D. beta of the transistor falls by 3 dB

5. A discone antenna is 5.____

   A. useful as for receiving UHF
   B. useful for direction-finding
   C. circularly polarized
   D. used for radar

6. Which of the following is UNLIKELY to be used as a pulsed device? 6.____

   A. CFA
   B. Multicavity klystron
   C. TWT
   D. BWO

7. A tunnel diode is loosely coupled to its cavity in order to 7.____

   A. facilitate tuning
   B. allow operation at the highest frequencies
   C. increase available negative resistance
   D. increase the frequency stability

8. Waveguides are used mainly for microwave signals because 8.____

   A. they depend on straight-line propagation
   B. they are too bulky at lower frequencies
   C. losses would be too great at lower frequencies
   D. generators cannot excite them at lower frequencies

9. Waveguides are used mainly for microwave signals because

    A. they depend on straight-line propagation
    B. they are too bulky at lower frequencies
    C. losses would be too great at lower frequencies
    D. generators cannot excite them at lower frequencies

10. Which of the following is NOT a disadvantage associated with the use of TDMA for providing multiple access to satellite communication systems?

    A. beamwidth   B. input capacitance
    C. bandwidth   D. effective height

11. Which type of *window signal* test can be used to read the peak-to-peak voltage of a video signal?

    A. Sync compression measurement
    B. Ringing indication
    C. Test and adjustment
    D. Continuity check

12. A basic group B in broadband communications

    A. consists of several erect channels only
    B. occupies the frequency range from 60 to 108 kHz
    C. consists of five supergroups
    D. is formed at the group translating equipment

13. Which type of modulation is normally recommended for use with a modem having a transmission rate of 14400 b/s?

    A. QAM   B. PSK   C. FSK   D. PCM

14. The orbital period of a typical geostationary satellite is _____ hours.

    A. 12   B. 24   C. 36   D. 48

15. For what reason is a three-holed directional coupler sometimes used in preference to the two-hole coupler?

    A. To reduce spurious mode generation
    B. To increase system bandwidth
    C. Because of greater efficiency
    D. To increase coupling of the signal

16. Almost all very high gain reflector antennas are of the _____ type.

    A. isotropic   B. dipole
    C. square-loop   D. Cassegrain

17. For most interexchange or long-distance optical fiber link, the fiber cable must contain a MINIMUM of _____ fibers.

    A. 2   B. 4   C. 6   D. 12

18. The IF bandwidth of a radar receiver is inversely proportional to the

    A. pulse interval
    B. square root of the peak transmitted power
    C. pulse repetition frequency
    D. pulse width

19. Zoning is used with a dielectric antenna to

    A. increase the bandwidth of the lens
    B. permit precise focusing
    C. correct the curvature of the wavefront
    D. reduce the bulk of the lens

20. Which of the following is NOT a type of active or closed-loop satellite tracking method?

    A. Feed scan   B. Monopulse
    C. Step-leak   D. Conscan

21. Which of the following is a problem associated PRIMARILY with the coupler crossbar switch matrix architecture used with processing satellites?

    A. High insertion loss
    B. Poor reliability
    C. Random interruptions
    D. Difficulty in maintaining isolation

22. EM waves acquire an apparent velocity greater than the velocity of light in space, due to reflections from a plane conducting wall.
    This phenomenon is termed _____ velocity.

    A. phase   B. group
    C. propagation   D. normal

23. Which of the following is NOT a method of bit-rate reduction used for digital television signals?

    A.
    B. Removal of composite input
    C. Reduction of sampling frequency
    D. Removal of horizontal and/or vertical blanking intervals
    E. Reduction of number of bits per sample

24. Each of the following is a measure that can be applied to optical communications systems to improve the link BER EXCEPT

    A. forward error correction
    B. star coupling
    C. equalization of polarization dispersion
    D. optical equalization of fiber chromatic dispersion

25. All of the following conditions must be met in order for a microwave transistor to operate at the highest frequencies EXCEPT the   25.____

    A. base should be thin
    B. emitter area must be large
    C. collector voltage must be large
    D. collector current must be high

KEY (CORRECT ANSWERS)

1.	A	11.	D
2.	B	12.	B
3.	B	13.	A
4.	C	14.	B
5.	A	15.	B
6.	D	16.	D
7.	D	17.	C
8.	B	18.	D
9.	A	19.	D
10.	D	20.	A

21. D
22. A
23. A
24. B
25. B

EXAMINATION SECTION
TEST 1

DIRECTIONS: Each question or incomplete statement is followed by several suggested answers or completions. Select the one that BEST answers the question or completes the statement. *PRINT THE LETTER OF THE CORRECT ANSWER IN THE SPACE AT THE RIGHT.*

1. Which of the following is MOST likely to be found in a single-sideband transmitter?   1.____

   A. Tuned modulator
   B. Class A RF output amplifier
   C. Class B RF amplifier
   D. Class C audio amplifier

2. If a parametric amplifier has an input and output frequency of 2.25 GHz and is pumped at 4.5 GHz, it is a(n)   2.____

   A. degenerate amplifier
   B. traveling-wave amplifier
   C. upper-sideband up converter
   D. lower-sideband up converter

3. Which of the following is exclusively a qualitative measure of an analog link or channel?   3.____

   A. Attenuation   B. Signal-to-noise ratio
   C. Amplification   D. Bit error ratio

4. Which of the following types of line terminal measurements performed on an optical fiber system is a check to ensure that no signal degradation has occurred over a period of time?   4.____

   A. Optical received power   B. BER
   C. Optical output power   D. Protection switching

5. A coaxial cable system is 100 km long and uses a .375 inch cable capable of transmitting up to 2700 VF channels in an FDM/SSB configuration. At 12 MHz, the cable attenuation per kilometer would be _____ dB.   5.____

   A. 4.15   B. 8.3   C. 415   D. 830

6. The approximate range of microwave transmission frequencies is   6.____

   A. 300-3400 kHz   B. 20-250 Hz
   C. 250-2000 MHz   D. 2-24 GHz

7. Which of the following is NOT a type of optical fiber currently in use?   7.____

   A. Step index   B. Graded index
   C. Pulse log   D. Single-mode

8. A maser RF amplifier is suitable for each of the following applications EXCEPT   8.____

   A. troposcatter receivers
   B. satellite communications

9

C. radioastronomy
D. radar

9. The difference between phase and frequency modulation is

    A. too large to make the two systems compatible
    B. due to differing definitions of the modulation index
    C. purely theoretical
    D. due to the poorer audio response of phase modulation

10. In analog facsimile systems, the signal-to-noise ratio at the receiver input should be dB or better.

    A. 5   B. 15   C. 30   D. 45 on

11. Surface acoustic waves propagate in

    A. quartz crystal   B. stripline
    C. indium phosphide   D. gallium arsenide

12. Which of the following is NOT an advantage associated with the use of FDMA for providing multiple access to satellite communication systems?

    A. Easy interface
    B. Mature technology
    C. Low IM in satellite transponder output
    D. No network timing requirement

13. Of the following factors, the _____ is NOT necessary to determine the gain of an isotropic antenna.

    A. effective area of aperture
    B. wavelength
    C. efficiency
    D. beamwidth

14. Which of the following is a problem associated PRIMARILY with the single pole/multiple throw switch matrix architecture used with processing satellites?

    A. High insertion loss
    B. High-input VSWR
    C. Random interruptions
    D. Difficulty in maintaining isolation

15. The _____ type of facsimile recording uses xerography techniques.

    A. electrothermal   B. electrolytic
    C. electropercussive   D. electrostatic

16. The purpose of companding is to

    A. protect small signals in PCM from quantizing distortion
    B. overcome impulse noise in PCM receivers
    C. overcome quantizing noise in PCM
    D. allow amplitude limiting in PCM receivers

17. Which of the following is an element particular to analog microwave radio systems? 17._____

    A. Frequency division multiplexer
    B. Antenna
    C. PSK modulator
    D. Mixer

18. Which of the following statements about satellite communication is TRUE? 18._____

    A. Collocated earth stations are used for frequency diversity.
    B. An earth station must have as many receive chains as there are carriers transmitted to it.
    C. If two earth stations do not face a common satellite, they should communicate via a double-satellite hop.
    D. Satellites in a system are allocated so that it is impossible for two earth stations not to face the same satellite.

19. A basic North American telephone channel between 500 and 2500 Hz, referenced to 1004 Hz, can expect the worst amplitude-frequency response to be from _____ dB of attenuation distortion. 19._____

    A. -8 to +6   B. -4 to +4
    C. -2 to +8   D. 0 to +5

20. Which of the following units for measuring power is used MOST widely with video transmissions? 20._____

    A. dB   B. dBm   C. dBW   D. dBmV

21. Cassegrain feed would be used with a parabolic reflector antenna in order to 21._____

    A. allow convenient placement of the feed
    B. increase the gain of the system
    C. reduce the size of the main reflector
    D. increase the beamwidth of the system

22. Which of the following levels or *layers* of the international technical standards for data transmission equipment is devoted to network architecture? 22._____

    A. Physical   B. Application
    C. Network control   D. Link

23. In an FM stereo multiplex transmission, the _____ signal modulates the _____ kHz subcarrier. 23._____

    A. difference; 19   B. difference; 38
    C. difference; 67   D. sum; 19

24. In fiber optic communication systems, which of the following devices are used at the output of LD sources to stop reflections from increasing the laser bandwidth? 24._____

    A. Filters   B. Amplifiers
    C. Couplers   D. Isolators

25. Ground waves eventually disappear as they move away from a transmitter because of   25.____
    A. tilting
    B. sky-wave interference
    C. loss of line-of-sight conditions
    D. maximum single-hop limitation

KEY (CORRECT ANSWERS)

1.	C	11.	A
2.	A	12.	C
3.	B	13.	D
4.	A	14.	C
5.	B	15.	D
6.	D	16.	A
7.	C	17.	A
8.	D	18.	B
9.	B	19.	C
10.	C	20.	D

21.	A
22.	B
23.	B
24.	D
25.	A

TEST 2

DIRECTIONS: Each question or incomplete statement is followed by several suggested answers or completions. Select the one that BEST answers the question or completes the statement. *PRINT THE LETTER OF THE CORRECT ANSWER IN THE SPACE AT THE RIGHT.*

1. The TWT is sometimes preferred to the multicavity klystron amplifier because it 1.____

    A. has a higher number of modes
    B. produces a higher output power
    C. has a greater bandwidth
    D. is more efficient

2. Which of the following is NOT a common method of attaining longer telephone subscriber loops without exceeding loss limits? 2.____

    A. Increasing conductor diameter
    B. Hybridization
    C. Amplifiers
    D. Inductive loading

3. If a receiver has poor IF selectivity, it will also have poor 3.____

    A. diversity reception   B. sensitivity
    C. double-spotting   D. blocking

4. Quantizing noise occurs in 4.____

    A. frequency-division multiplex
    B. pulse-code modulation
    C. time-division multiplex
    D. pulse-width modulation

5. If the antenna current of an AM system is doubled when the modulation index of the wave is doubled, the AM system being used is 5.____

    A. single sideband, full carrier
    B. single sideband, suppressed carrier
    C. double-sideband, full carrier
    D. vestigial sideband

6. Which type of cellular radio system uses a single carrier modulated by the speech signals of many users? 6.____

    A. Digital FDMA   B. Digital narrowband TDMA
    C. Analog FM   D. Digital wideband

7. Which of the following methods would NOT serve to combat noise in a digital system? 7.____

    A. Using redundancy
    B. Increasing transmitted power
    C. Increasing channel bandwidth
    D. Reducing signaling rate

8. Of the following, the _____ type of filters is MOST commonly used in SSB generation.

   A. low-pass
   B. mechanical
   C. RC
   D. LC

9. For what reason would a choke flange be used to couple two waveguides?

   A. To compensate for discontinuities at the joint
   B. To help in the alignment of the waveguides
   C. To increase the bandwidth of the system
   D. Relative simplicity compared to other joins

10. Each of the following is a method for controlling echo in a telephone signal EXCEPT

    A. improved return loss at the term set
    B. freeing passage for reflected signal energy
    C. reducing gain of individual four-wire amplifiers
    D. adding loss on the four-wire side

11. As the noise sideband frequency of an FM wave approaches the carrier frequency, the noise amplitude

    A. remains constant
    B. is decreased
    C. is equalized
    D. is increased

12. Which of the following is NOT true of the use of component coding in the transmission of digital television signals?

    A. Country receiving signal via an international circuit uses a different color system from the source country
    B. Output to the receiving circuit is in composite form
    C. It is a method adopted generally for studios
    D. Transmission path is entirely digital

13. The baud rate in digital communications is

    A. not equal to the signaling rate
    B. equal to one-half the bandwidth of an ideal channel
    C. equal to twice the bandwidth of an ideal channel
    D. always equal to the bit transfer rate

14. Which of the following is NOT a disadvantage associated with the use of geostationary satellite networks in comnunications?

    A. No polar coverage
    B. Transmission delay
    C. Free space loss
    D. Excessive Doppler shift

15. Cylindrical cavity resonators are NOT used with klystrons because of

    A. too great losses
    B. harmonically related resonant frequencies
    C. too low Q
    D. difficulty in calculating resonant frequency, because of shape

16. The circuit that separates sync pulses from a composite video waveform is called a(n)

    A. clipper
    B. integrator
    C. keyed AGC amplifier
    D. differentiator

17. What is the typical gauge of telephone cable used for long distance communication?

    A. 12   B. 19   C. 24   D. 30

18. The term for the signals sent by a TV transmitter to ensure correct scanning in the receiver is

    A. luminance   B. video   C. chroma   D. sync

19. A communication network has three networks in series. The first is an attenuator with a 12-dB loss; the second is an amplifier with a 35-dB gain, and the third has an insertion loss of 10 dB.
    If the input at the first device is 4W, the output of the last device is _____ W.

    A. .08   B. 13   C. 80   D. 130

20. In North America, a digital multiplexer packages channels in groups of

    A. 18   B. 24   C. 30   D. 42

21. What is the MAIN disadvantage associated with the use of an IMPATT diode?

    A. High noise
    B. Inability to provide pulsed operation
    C. Lower efficiency than other microwave diodes
    D. Low power-handling ability

22. Which of the following is NOT an advantage associated with the use of a phase discriminator over a slope detector?

    A. Fewer tuned circuits
    B. Easier alignment
    C. Better linearity
    D. Greater limiting

23. Manganese ferrite may NOT be used as a(n)

    A. garnet
    B. isolator
    C. phase shifter
    D. circulator

24. The output of the vertical amplifier, applied to the yoke in a television receiver, consists of

    A. DC
    B. a sawtooth current
    C. amplified vertical sync pulses
    D. a sawtooth voltage

25. When using QAM to modulate a digital radio signal, additional carrier-to-noise degradation is likely to be caused by each of the following EXCEPT

    A. thermal noise
    B. amplitude distortion
    C. timing error
    D. delay distortion

KEY (CORRECT ANSWERS)

1. C
2. B
3. D
4. B
5. B

6. D
7. C
8. B
9. A
10. B

11. B
12. B
13. C
14. D
15. B

16. A
17. B
18. D
19. A
20. B

21. A
22. D
23. A
24. B
25. A

EXAMINATION SECTION
TEST 1

DIRECTIONS: Each question or incomplete statement is followed by several suggested answers or completions. Select the one that BEST answers the question or completes the statement. *PRINT THE LETTER OF THE CORRECT ANSWER IN THE SPACE AT THE RIGHT.*

1. In telephone systems, grade-of-service is measured as a function of   1.____

    A. return loss at sampled term sets
    B. proportion of calls in a circuit-switched network which are lost owing to congestion
    C. the mean reference equivalent of all subscriber loops
    D. signal-to-noise ratio in sample subscriber loops

2. Each of the following is an advantage associated with the use of an LD over an LED in optical transmission systems EXCEPT   2.____

    A. wider bandwidth
    B. higher output power
    C. immunity to reflective light
    D. narrow spectrum

3. Because of fading and increase in antenna noise, elevation angles of geostationary satellites are undesirable below _____°.   3.____

    A. 5   B. 15   C. 30   D. 45

4. Which of the following terms applies to troposcatter propagation?   4.____

    A. Faraday rotation   B. SIDs
    C. Atmospheric storms   D. Fading

5. Of the following diodes, the _____ is suitable ONLY for very low-power oscillators.   5.____

    A. avalanche   B. IMPATT   C. Gunn   D. tunnel

6. Each of the following is a noise-component to be considered in a coaxial cable system EXCEPT _____ noise.   6.____

    A. first-order IM   B. second-order IM
    C. third-order IM   D. thermal

7. The PRIMARY method used to provide multiple access to a satellite communication network is   7.____

    A. analog FM   B. FDMA   C. TDMA   D. CDMA

8. When traveling through a typical PCM transmitter, which phase of speech output would a voice signal encounter LAST?   8.____

    A. Decoding   B. Hold circuit
    C. Sampling   D. Low-pass filter

9. Long-haul optical fiber systems must use _____ fibers. 9.____

   A. silica multimode
   B. plastic
   C. zinc-based
   D. single-mode

10. An ungrounded antenna placed near the ground 10.____

    A. acts as an antenna array
    B. is unlikely to need an earth mat
    C. acts as a single antenna of twice the height
    D. must be horizontally polarized

11. If an AM receiver uses a diode detector for demodulation, it will be able to satisfactorily receive 11.____

    A. ISB
    B. single-sideband, full carrier
    C. single-sideband, suppressed carrier
    D. single-sideband, reduced carrier

12. The noise temperature of an antenna may be determined by all of the following factors EXCEPT 12.____

    A. loss between antenna and receiver output
    B. reflection
    C. sky noise from sun, moon, and stars
    D. absorption by atmosphere and precipitation

13. In the United States television system, the intercarrier frequency is _____ MHz. 13.____

    A. 4.5   B. 6   C. 12   D. 14.5

14. Which of the following is NOT one of the most important physical aspects of optical fiber material? 14.____

    A. Attenuation
    B. Numerical aperture
    C. Core diameter
    D. Dispersion

15. The purpose of the attenuator in a traveling-wave tube is to 15.____

    A. help bunching
    B. prevent saturation
    C. increase gain
    D. prevent oscillations

16. A technician performs a line terminal measurement on an optical fiber system by attaching an electrical input to the LTE from a pattern generator, and then adding an optical-to-electrical converter to the output line. 16.____
    Which measurement is being performed?

    A. Optical received power
    B. BER
    C. Optical output power
    D. Optical output pulse waveform

17. Pulse-width modulation may be generated

    A. with a monostable multivibrator
    B. by integrating the signal
    C. with a free-running multivibrator
    D. by differentiating pulse-position modulation

18. Which of the following modulation techniques for digital radio signals uses phase reversal every time a binary coded *1* in the bit stream changes to a *0*?

    A. QAM   B. FSK   C. PSK   D. PAM

19. The input to a network is .0004 W. What is the input measured in dBm?

    A. -4   B. .04   C. 1.2   D. 12

20. Using uniform quantization in a frequency modulation system, what would be the APPROXIMATE signal-to-noise ratio if the system were encoded with an 8-bit binary code word?

    A. 44   B. 50   C. 62   D. 74

21. A cavity magnetron uses strapping to

    A. improve the phase-focusing effect
    B. prevent mode-jumping
    C. prevent cathode back-heating
    D. ensure bunching

22. In fiber optic systems, _____ dB of isolation are required in order to ensure that reflections are adequately reduced.

    A. 10-20   B. 30-40   C. 50-60   D. 70-80

23. Which of the following is NOT a method of synchronization used with conventional analog facsimile systems?

    A. Tying both machines to a common AC power source frequency
    B. System operation with synchronizing signals during transmission
    C. Replication of amplifier placement along each transmission line
    D. Operation of each machine with a stabilized frequency power source

24. The purpose of serrations in the composite video waveform is to

    A. help horizontal synchronization
    B. simplify generation of the vertical sync pulse
    C. help vertical synchronization
    D. equalize the charge in the integrator before the start of the vertical retrace

25. Which of the following types of antenna is circularly polarized?

    A. Parabolic reflector   B. Yagi-Uda
    C. Helical   D. Small circular loop

KEY (CORRECT ANSWERS)

1. B
2. C
3. A
4. D
5. D

6. A
7. B
8. D
9. D
10. A

11. B
12. B
13. A
14. C
15. D

16. D
17. A
18. C
19. A
20. B

21. B
22. C
23. C
24. A
25. C

———

TEST 2

DIRECTIONS: Each question or incomplete statement is followed by several suggested answers or completions. Select the one that BEST answers the question or completes the statement. *PRINT THE LETTER OF THE CORRECT ANSWER IN THE SPACE AT THE RIGHT.*

1. Coaxial cable should be considered in lieu of radiolinks out of hand in all of the following situations EXCEPT

    A. on high-density routes where it may be more economical
    B. in areas already containing heavily loaded ducting
    C. in areas of heavy microwave RFI
    D. on long or international backbone routes where the designer is concerned with noise accumulation

    1.____

2. A telephone cable with a diameter of .32 mm has a mutual capacitance of 40 nF/km and a loop resistance of 433 ft/km. Its attenuation at 1000 kHz would be _____ dB/km.

    A. .44   B. .92   C. 1.30   D. 2.03

    2.____

3. In a communication system, the modulation index is halved and the modulating voltage remains constant when the modulating frequency is doubled.
Which modulation system is being used?

    A. Phase   B. Frequency   C. Amplitude   D. All of the above

    3.____

4. Which of the following is used to locate breaks in an optical fiber cable?

    A. HRC   B. OTDR   C. VOGAD   D. STS

    4.____

5. Which of the following frequencies CANNOT be used for reliable beyond-the-horizon terrestrial communications without repeaters?

    A. 25 kHz   B. 20 MHz   C. 1000 MHz   D. 12 GHz

    5.____

6. A TOT is sometimes preferred to the magnetron as a radar transmitter output tube because it is

    A. less noisy
    C. more broadband
    B. a more efficient amplifier
    D. capable of a longer duty cycle

    6.____

7. Which of the following is NOT a type of satellite commonly used in communication systems?

    A. Equatorial   B. Inclined   C. Superlunar   D. Polar

    7.____

8. Of the following, an ADVANTAGE associated with the use of base modulation over collector modulation of a transistor class C amplifier is

    A. better linearity
    B. lower modulating power requirement
    C. better efficiency
    D. higher power output per transistor

    8.____

9. The unigauge system of designing telephone subscriber loops typically allows most of the longest loops to use _____-gauge conductors.

   A. 12 B. 19 C. 26 D. 32

10. Each of the following is a type of omnidirectional antenna EXCEPT

   A. Marconi B. discone
   C. log-periodic D. half-wave dipole

11. A scheme in which several channels are interleaved and then transmitted together is called a

   A. group
   B. supergroup
   C. frequency-division multiplex
   D. time-division multiplex

12. What is the width of the vertical sync pulse in the United States television system?

   A. H B. .5H C. 3H D. 21H

13. Magnetic wave polarization

   A. is always vertical in an isotropic medium
   B. is caused by reflection
   C. is due to the transverse nature of the wave
   D. results from the longitudinal nature of the wave

14. Which of the following is NOT a type of waveguide?

   A. Coaxial B. Ridged C. Elliptical D. Flexible

15. The optical fiber dispersion that is MOST significant in single-mode fibers is the _____ type.

   A. modal B. material
   C. waveguide D. multimodal

16. Which method of testing for video quality is used for a quick check of gain at a few determined frequencies?

   A. Sine-squared signal B. Stair steps
   C. VITS D. Multiburst

17. In PCM systems, what is the term for using an output channel whose bit rate is purposely higher than the input bit rate?

   A. Pulse stuffing B. Line coding
   C. Mark inversion D. Companding

3 (#2)

18. Vacuum tubes eventually fail at microwave frequencies because of 18._____
    A. decreasing series inductive reactance
    B. shortening transmit time
    C. increasing shunt capacitance
    D. increasing noise figure

19. The standard reference antenna for the directive gain is the 19._____
    A. elementary doublet   B. isotropic antenna
    C. half-wave dipole   D. infinitesimal dipole

Questions 20-25.

DIRECTIONS: Questions 20 through 25 are to be answered on the basis of the diagram of a horn reflector antenna shown below. Place the letter that corresponds to each diagrammed component in the space at the right.

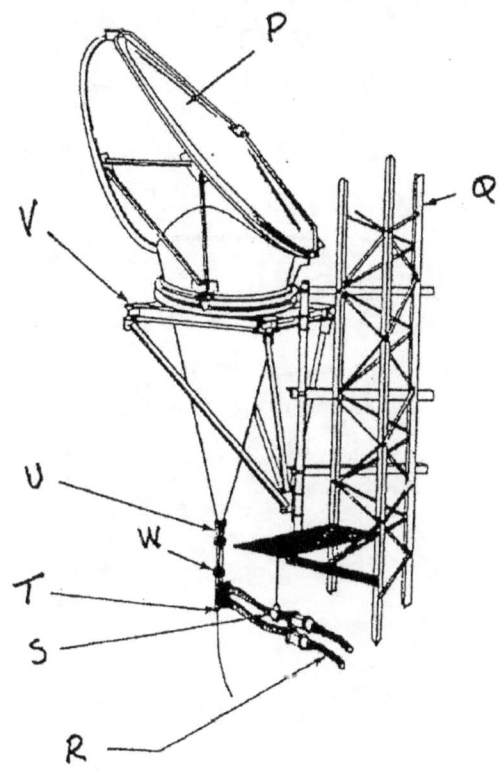

20. Antenna mount 20._____

21. Dual-polarized circular to rectangular transition 21._____

22. Flex-twist and hanger 22._____

23. Network drain 23._____

24. Taper transition 24._____

25. Elliptical waveguide system 25._____

KEY (CORRECT ANSWERS)

1.	B		11.	C
2.	D		12.	C
3.	B		13.	C
4.	B		14.	A
5.	D		15.	C
6.	D		16.	D
7.	C		17.	A
8.	B		18.	D
9.	C		19.	B
10.	C		20.	V

21. W
22. S
23. T
24. U
25. R

EXAMINATION SECTION
TEST 1

DIRECTIONS: Each question or incomplete statement is followed by several suggested answers or completions. Select the one that BEST answers the question or completes the statement. *PRINT THE LETTER OF THE CORRECT ANSWER IN THE SPACE AT THE RIGHT.*

1. _____ levels or *layers* of the international technical standards for data transmission equipment provides addressing information to guide data from the sender terminal to receiver location.

    A. Link
    B. Session
    C. Network control
    D. Presentation

    1.____

2. Of the following, a PRIMARY function of the RF amplifier in a superheterodyne receiver is to

    A. permit better adjacent-channel rejection
    B. increase the tuning range of the receiver
    C. improve the rejection of the image frequency
    D. provide improved tracking

    2.____

3. When using uniform quantization to achieve the speech range standard in a transmitting system, the number of bits per code word should be AT LEAST

    A. 7   B. 10   C. 12   D. 14

    3.____

4. The sound of a talker's voice heard in his/her own telephone receiver is termed

    A. feedback
    B. singing
    C. distortion
    D. sidetone

    4.____

5. Which of the following would result from a LOW ratio of AC to DC load impedance in a diode detector?

    A. Negative-peak clipping
    B. Poor AF response
    C. Poor AGC operation
    D. Diagonal clipping

    5.____

6. Of the following, the LAST block of the synchronous digital hierarchy (SDH) multiplexing structure is the

    A. tributary unit group
    B. synchronous transport module
    C. container
    D. virtual tributary

    6.____

7. Which of the following is an impairment causing amplitude errors on data transmission lines?

    A. Phase hits
    B. Frequency response
    C. Gain hits
    D. Pulse distortion

    7.____

8. Which of the following would NOT show up on a received facsimile transmission picture as a herringbone pattern?

   A. Phase jitter
   B. Echo
   C. Crosstalk
   D. Single-frequency interference

9. According to the present North American telephone subscriber loop design rules, a loop using the RRD design parameter must have a loop resistance of

   A. 1300 Ω maximum
   B. 1301-3600 Ω
   C. 1501-2800 Ω
   D. 0-2800 Ω

10. Which of the following modulation techniques for digital radio signals allocates one fixed frequency tone for the binary *1*'s and another tone for *0*'s?

    A. QAM
    B. FSK
    C. PSK
    D. PAM

11. Which of the following would NOT be used to couple two generators to a waveguide system without coupling them to each other?

    A. E-plane T
    B. Hybrid ring
    C. Rat-race
    D. Magic T

12. When the subspectra of a sampled signal overlap with each other, resulting in the loss of information about the original source signal, a phenomenon known as _____ occurs.

    A. ghosting
    B. companding
    C. aliasing distortion
    D. temporal noise

13. The velocity factor of a transmission line

    A. is higher for a solid dielectric than for air
    B. is governed by the skin effect
    C. increases the velocity along the transmission line
    D. depends on the dielectric constant of the material used

14. Which type of *window signal* test can be used to compare locally received video window signals with those transmitted from the distant end?

    A. Sync compression measurement
    B. Ringing indication
    C. Test and adjustment
    D. Continuity check.

15. Of the following, the _____ is NOT a useful quantity for comparing the noise performance of receivers.

    A. noise temperature
    B. input noise voltage
    C. noise figure
    D. equivalent noise resistance

16. In a communications system, noise is MOST likely to affect the signal 16._____
    A. in the channel
    B. at the transmitter
    C. in the information source
    D. at the destination

Questions 17-25.

DIRECTIONS: Questions 17 through 25 are to be answered on the basis of the cross-section diagram of an optical fiber cable shown below. Place the letter that corresponds to each diagrammed component in the space at the right.

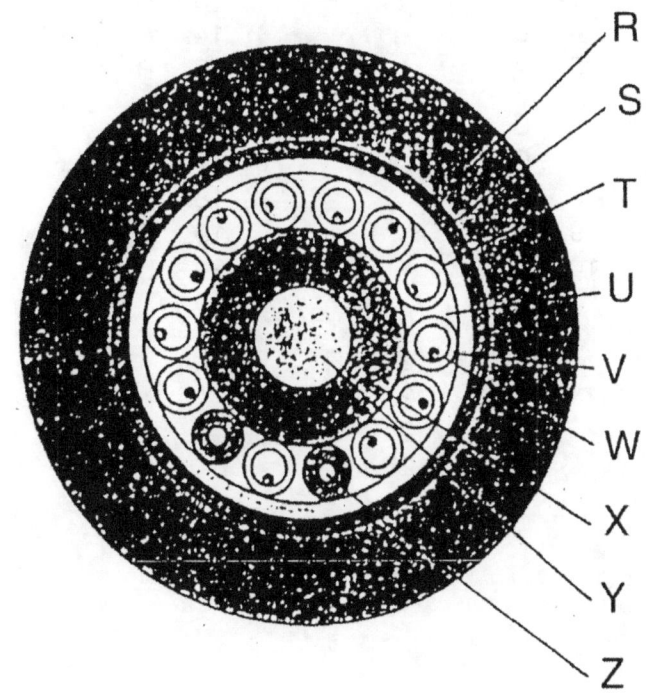

17. Buffer tube 17._____
18. Strength members of aramide yarn 18._____
19. Fiber 19._____
20. Core-filling compound 20._____
21. All-dielectric support element 21._____
22. Polyethylene jacket 22._____
23. Copper conductor 23._____

4 (#1)

24. Barrier layer   24._____
25. Buffer   25._____

KEY (CORRECT ANSWERS)

1.	C		11.	A
2.	C		12.	C
3.	C		13.	D
4.	D		14.	A
5.	A		15.	B
6.	B		16.	A
7.	C		17.	V
8.	B		18.	T
9.	A		19.	W
10.	B		20.	U

21. Y
22. R
23. Z
24. S
25. X

TEST 2

DIRECTIONS: Each question or incomplete statement is followed by several suggested answers or completions. Select the one that BEST answers the question or completes the statement. *PRINT THE LETTER OF THE CORRECT ANSWER IN THE SPACE AT THE RIGHT.*

Questions 1-8.

DIRECTIONS: Questions 1 through 8 are to be answered on the basis of the diagram of a technician's setup for an output waveform measurement with an optical line terminal shown below. Place the letter that corresponds to each diagrammed component in the space at the right.

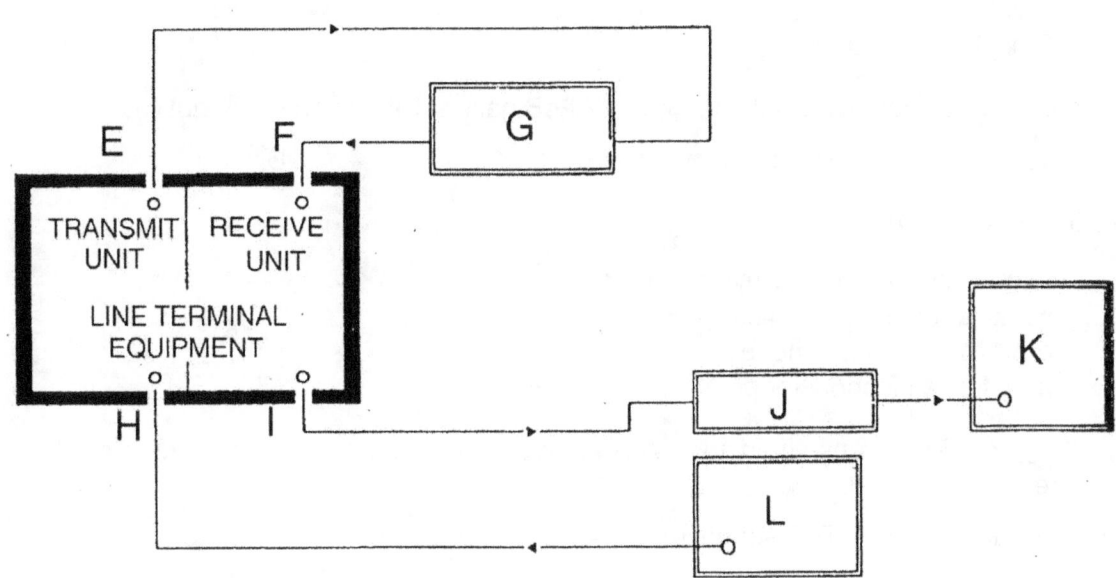

1. Digital output   1.____
2. Variable attenuator   2.____
3. Optical input   3.____
4. Pattern generator   4.____
5. Digital input   5.____
6. Oscilloscope   6.____
7. Optical output   7.____
8. Attenuator   8.____
9. The purpose of Kevlar in optical fibers is to   9.____
   A. provide longitudinal strength
   B. aid in jointing

29

C. prevent noise accumulation
D. guard against surveillance

10. The type of cavity structure used in the magnetron to avoid difficulties with strapping at high frequencies is the

    A. vane
    B. rising sun
    C. slot
    D. hole-and-slot

11. Which type of cellular radio system resembles analog FM, but with a carrier that is modulated by digitally encoded speech signals?

    A. Digital FDMA
    B. Digital narrowband TDMA
    C. CDMA
    D. Digital wideband

12. If the input to a microwave network with a 20-dB gain is 1 W, its output in dbW is

    A. 19
    B. 20
    C. 21
    D. 40

13. A PIN diode is NOT

    A. often used as a microwave detector
    B. suitable for use as a microwave switch
    C. a microwave mixer mode
    D. a metal semiconductor point-contact diode

14. A _____ carrier is transmitted 1.25 MHz above the bottom frequency in a US television channel.

    A. picture
    B. sound
    C. chroma
    D. inter

15. Which of the following is used to provide 2-wire to 4-wire transmission line conversion in a telephone subscriber loop?

    A. Term set
    B. Hybrid
    C. Three-hole coupler
    D. Bidirectional coupler

16. The PRIMARY advantage of overhead optical fiber installation over underground is

    A. greater safety in installation and maintenance
    B. relatively lower risk of disruption
    C. lower maintenance expense
    D. lower installation expense

17. Which of the following CANNOT be used to demodulate single-sideband transmissions?

    A. Complete phase-shift generator
    B. Diode balanced modulator
    C. Product detector
    D. Bipolar transistor balanced modulator

18. The length of a wave in a waveguide

    A. depends only on the waveguide dimensions and the free-space wavelength
    B. is inversely proportional to the phase velocity

C. is greater than in free space
D. is directly proportional to the group velocity

19. For the BEST low-level noise performance in the X-band, an amplifier should use a(n) 19.____

    A. step-recovery diode B. IMPATT diode
    C. bipolar transistor D. Gunn diode

20. Which of the following transmission systems uses two ground planes? 20.____

    A. Stripline B. Elliptical waveguide
    C. Microstrip D. Parallel-wire line

21. Of the following, the _____ level of the international technical standards for data trans- 21.____
    mission equipment is concerned with the end-to-end message conveyance.

    A. presentation B. transport
    C. link D. session

22. The stability of a telephone connection depends on all of the following EXCEPT 22.____

    A. variation of transmission level with time
    B. distribution of balance return loss
    C. gain differential between links
    D. attenuation-frequency characteristic of the links in tandem

23. Which of the following waveguide tuning components is MOST difficult to adjust? 23.____

    A. Iris B. Stub C. Plunger D. Screw

24. If the power output of a laser is monochromatic, this means that it is also 24.____

    A. single-frequency B. narrow-beam
    C. infrared D. polarized

25. A sine-squared test signal is NOT used to evaluate the _____ of a video transmission. 25.____

    A. phase B. transient response
    C. envelope delay D. differential gain

KEY (CORRECT ANSWERS)

1. I
2. G
3. F
4. L
5. H

6. K
7. E
8. J
9. A
10. B

11. A
12. B
13. B
14. A
15. B

16. D
17. D
18. C
19. B
20. A

21. B
22. C
23. A
24. A
25. D

EXAMINATION SECTION
TEST 1

DIRECTIONS: Each question or incomplete statement is followed by several suggested answers or completions. Select the one that BEST answers the question or completes the statement. *PRINT THE LETTER OF THE CORRECT ANSWER IN THE SPACE AT THE RIGHT.*

1. The local oscillator of a broadcast receiver is tuned to a frequency higher than the incoming frequency in order to   1._____

    A. allow adequate frequency coverage without switching
    B. produce an otherwise impossible intermediate frequency
    C. help the image frequency rejection
    D. permit easier tracking

2. Routing within a local area network, or LAN, is performed by a switch known as a(n)   2._____

    A. GTE   B. MFC   C. VCO   D. PBX

3. Which of the following is NOT an advantage associated with the use of geostationary satellite network in communications?   3._____

    A. Nearly constant range
    B. No handover problem
    C. Simple ground station tracking
    D. Full global coverage

4. A system transmitting speech signals must be able to accommodate signals of AT LEAST a _____ -dB range.   4._____

    A. 20   B. 40   C. 60   D. 80

5. Which of the following types of noise disturbances in a communications circuit is caused by the products of two or nore signals mixing together?   5._____

    A. Thermal noise   B. Intermodulation noise
    C. Impulse noise   D. Crosstalk

6. Analog samples are USUALLY classified through a process known as   6._____

    A. modulation   B. quantizing
    C. framing   D. metering

7. What is the term for transmitting a continuous analog wave as an equivalent digital code?   7._____

    A. PCM   B. DSI   C. PBX   D. DTM

8. What is the term for the combined multiple-voice, data and/or video channels which are to be transmitted over a system?   8._____

    A. Broadband   B. Multiplex
    C. Baseband   D. Pulse code

9. The PRIMARY purpose of the helix in a traveling-wave tube is to

   A. reduce the noise figure
   B. ensure broadband operation
   C. reduce the axial velocity of the RF field
   D. prevent the electron beam from spreading in the long tube

10. The MOST important characteristic of microwave antennas is

    A. beamwidth   B. polarization
    C. radiation pattern   D. gain

11. Each of the following is a factor in the selection of either LD or LED for an optical transmission system EXCEPT

    A. numerical aperture   B. coupling efficiency
    C. spectral width   D. modulation type

12. When quantizing telephone signals, the range of signals is USUALLY divided into _____ intervals.

    A. 64   B. 128   C. 256   D. 512

13. If the SWR on a transmission line is infinity, the line will be terminated by each of the following EXCEPT a(n)

    A. pure reactance   B. open circuit
    C. complex impedance D. short circuit

14. The MAJOR differences between analog and digital microwave radios lie primarily within each of the following parameters EXCEPT

    A. baseband composition
    B. subscriber signal level
    C. service channel transmission
    D. modulation techniques

15. A parametric amplifier must be cooled in order to

    A. improve its noise performance
    B. make parametric amplification safer
    C. take it below room temperature
    D. increase its bandwidth

16. Which type of modulation is NORMALLY recommended for use with a modem having a transmission rate of 4800 b/s?

    A. QAM   B. PSK   C. FSK   D. PCM

17. In the United States, bandwidths are divided into administrative units of _____ Mb/second.

    A. 44.51   B. 51.84   C. 100.56   D. 155.52

18. Which of the following is a problem associated PRIMARILY with the fan-in/fan-out switch matrix architecture used with processing satellites?   18._____

    A. High insertion loss
    B. Difficult broadbanding
    C. Random interruptions
    D. Difficulty in maintaining isolation

19. In the regeneration of a digital signal, the threshold between two signal value ranges is known as the   19._____

    A. reconstructed sample   B. decision value
    C. virtual value   D. uniform value

20. Traveling-wave parametric amplifiers are used to   20._____

    A. reduce the number of required varactor diodes
    B. provide a greater bandwidth
    C. avoid the need for cooling
    D. provide a greater gain

21. Which of the following is TRUE of a typical squelch circuit? It   21._____

    A. eliminates RF interference in weak signals
    B. cuts off an IF amplifier when the AGC is at maximum
    C. cuts off an IF amplifier when the AGC is at minimum
    D. cuts off an audio amplifier when the carrier is absent

22. Which type of optical fiber dispersion is dependent ONLY on the dimensions of the fiber itself?   22._____

    A. Modal   B. Material
    C. Waveguide   D. Multimodal

23. The type of cellular radio system that uses one carrier for several customers is the   23._____

    A. digital FDMA
    B. digital narrowband TDMA
    C. CDMA
    D. digital wideband

24. Which of the following is an indirect means of generating frequency modulation?   24._____

    A. Reactance bipolar transistor modulator
    B. Varactor diode modulator
    C. Reactance FET modulator
    D. Armstrong modulator

25. A piston attenuator is a   25._____

    A. mode filter   B. vane attenuator
    C. waveguide below cutoff   D. flap attenuator

KEY (CORRECT ANSWERS)

1. A
2. D
3. D
4. C
5. B

6. B
7. A
8. C
9. C
10. D

11. A
12. C
13. C
14. B
15. A

16. B
17. B
18. A
19. B
20. B

21. D
22. A
23. B
24. D
25. C

TEST 2

DIRECTIONS: Each question or incomplete statement is followed by several suggested answers or completions. Select the one that BEST answers the question or completes the statement. *PRINT THE LETTER OF THE CORRECT ANSWER IN THE SPACE AT THE RIGHT.*

1. An AM facsimile signal requires an information bandwidth of about _____ Hz.

    A. 300 B. 800 C. 1400 D. 2100

2. Which of the following levels or *layers* of the international technical standards for data transmission equipment can establish the type of link to be set up? _____ level.

    A. Session
    B. Application
    C. Network control
    D. Link

3. In a satellite system, the propagation delay involved in the earth-to-satellite-to-earth signal path is APPROXIMATELY _____ second(s).

    A. .25 B. .5 C. 1 D. 3

4. Which of the following is NOT a parameter normally used to technically describe telephone channels?

    A. Level
    B. Amplitude modulation
    C. Phase distortion
    D. Nominal bandwidth

5. Each of the following is a parameter determining the design of an optical fiber link EXCEPT

    A. total link length
    B. bit rate
    C. error performance
    D. transmitted power

6. Which type of *window signal* test uses calibrated wide-band oscilloscopes to help adjust the horizontal scales of a video signal?

    A. Sync compression measurement
    B. Ringing indication
    C. Test and adjustment
    D. Continuity check

7. For which of the following reasons might a controlled oscillator synthesizer sometimes be preferred to a direct one?

    A. Better frequency stability
    B. No crystal oscillator requirement
    C. Relative freedom from spurious frequencies
    D. Simplicity of operation

8. A telephone subscriber's loop is a wire pair that USUALLY supplies a metallic path for each of the following EXCEPT

    A. ac ringing voltage
    B. an ac access current activated by uncradling of the instrument

37

C. talk battery for the transmitter
D. the dial which makes and breaks dc current in the closed loop

9. A backward-wave oscillator is based on the

   A. coaxial magnetron
   B. traveling-wave tube
   C. crossed-field amplifier
   D. rising-sun magnetron

10. Modulation is NOT used to

    A. ensure transmission over long distances
    B. allow the use of practicable antennas
    C. reduce the bandwidth used
    D. separate differing transmissions

11. The voltage of a telephone battery has been standardized at _____ V.

    A. -48 B. -24 C. 12 D. 18

12. For what reason is a helical antenna used for satellite tracking?

    A. Broad bandwidth
    B. Front-to-back ratio
    C. Circular polarization
    D. Maneuverability

13. What is the term for the angle of a satellite terminal antenna, measured from the horizontal to the point on the center of the main antenna beam when the beam is pointed directly at the satellite?

    A. Azimuth
    B. Look angle
    C. Equivalent angle
    D. Inclination

14. The standard bandwidth (Hz) for voice channels in a digital PCM transmission system is

    A. 150-1200 B. 200-2400 C. 300-3400 D. 500-1500

15. A duplexer is used to

    A. allow one antenna to be used for reception or transmission without mutual interference
    B. prevent interference between two antennas when they are connected to a receiver
    C. increase the speed of pulses in pulsed radar
    D. couple two different antennas to a transmitter without mutual interference

16. In the United States, which of the following is the FIRST block of the synchronous digital hierarchy (SDH) multiplexing structure?

    A. Tributary unit group
    B. Synchronous transport module
    C. Container
    D. Virtual tributary

17. The axial magnetic field and radial electric field of a microwave tube amplifier compose the

    A. traveling-wave magnetron
    B. CFA
    C. coaxial magnetron
    D. reflex klystron

18. For what reason are helical antennas often used for satellite tracking at VHF?

    A. Troposcatter
    B. Faraday effect
    C. Ionospheric refraction
    D. Superrefraction

19. The major quality improvement obtained in digital transmission systems is due PRIMARILY to

    A. signal-to-noise ratios
    B. receiver signal recovery techniques
    C. a capacity for more complex basebands
    D. multiplexing

20. With rectangular waveguides, the dominant mode of propagation is preferred for each of the following reasons EXCEPT

    A. it is easier to excite than other modes
    B. propagation without any spurious generation can be ensured
    C. the resulting impedance can be matched directly to coaxial lines
    D. it leads to the smallest waveguide dimensions.

21. Impedance inversion in a transmission line may be obtained with a(n)

    A. quarter-wave line
    B. half-wave line
    C. open-circuited stub
    D. short-circuited stub

22. When traveling through a typical PCM transmitter, which phase of speech input would a voice signal encounter LAST?

    A. Encoding
    B. A/D conversion
    C. Sampling
    D. Low-pass filter

23.
24. Frequencies in the UHF range normally propagate by means of _____ waves.

    A. surface   B. sky   C. space   D. ground

25. In a telephone system, which of the following codes for load coil spacing is used LEAST frequently?

    A. B   B. D   C. H   D. X

26. Of the following modulation techniques for digital radio signals, a linear technique for improving bandwidth efficiency is

    A. QAM   B. FSK   C. PSK   D. PAM

KEY (CORRECT ANSWERS)

1. C
2. A
3. A
4. B
5. D

6. B
7. C
8. B
9. B
10. C

11. A
12. C
13. B
14. C
15. A

16. C
17. B
18. B
19. B
20. C

21. A
22. A
23. C
24. D
25. D

TEST 2

DIRECTIONS: Each question or incomplete statement is followed by several suggested answers or completions. Select the one that BEST answers the question or completes the statement. *PRINT THE LETTER OF THE CORRECT ANSWER IN THE SPACE AT THE RIGHT.*

1. Fast Ethernet can run on
   A. UTP
   B. optical fiber
   C. wireless
   D. all of the above

   1.____

2. Fiber fast Ethernet can provide speeds of up to
   A. 1 GBPS   B. 512 MBPS   C. 100 MBPS   D. 256 KBPS

   2.____

3. Giga-Ethernet provides speed up to _____ MBPS over fiber.
   A. 1000   B. 512   C. 256   D. 1.5

   3.____

4. _____ LAN is a solution to divide a single broadcast domain into multiple broadcast domains.
   A. Virtual   B. Localized   C. Bridged   D. Broadcast

   4.____

5. Internet uses _____ topology.
   A. hybrid   B. daisy chain   C. dual ring   D. mesh

   5.____

6. Unlike OSI, the Internet model uses _____ layers.
   A. 3   B. 4   C. 7   D. 5

   6.____

7. Infrared frequency ranges from 300 GHz to 43 THz and is used for
   A. TV remotes
   B. penetrating obstacles
   C. communications of up to 1000 meters
   D. line of sight communication

   7.____

8. Frequency Division Multiplexing (FDM) uses _____ to distribute bandwidth.
   A. frequency   B. channels   C. time slots   D. path

   8.____

9. _____ is used to provide abstraction of services.
   A. Abstraction layer
   B. Network layer
   C. Encapsulation
   D. Collision detection

   9.____

10. _____ are addressed via ports.
    A. Processes
    B. Memory address
    C. NIC
    D. Protocols

    10.____

11. SMTP is _____-level protocol.
    A. higher   B. lower   C. user   D. network

12. _____ layer provides host-to-host communications.
    A. Network   B. Data   C. Transport   D. Physical

13. _____ is basic transport layer protocol.
    A. UDP   B. HTTP   C. HTTPS   D. FTP

14. Adding a packet header is a function of
    A. transport   B. physical   C. data link   D. application

15. _____ requires sending from one network to another.
    A. Internetworking   B. Transmission control
    C. TCP   D. IP

16. A host is identified using
    A. IP addressing system   B. website address
    C. MAC address   D. Checksum

17. 128-bit addressing is made possible by
    A. IPV4   B. IPV6   C. TCP/IP   D. UDP

18. HDLC stands for
    A. High Level Link Control   B. High Level Data Level Checking
    C. High Definition Latency Check   D. High Definition Least Control

19. IP (Internet Protocol) does NOT guarantee _____ delivery.
    A. reliable   B. efficient   C. error-free   D. complete

20. Routers and _____ do not examine traffic.
    A. graphic cards   B. bridges
    C. network hubs   d switches

21. A PAN may use _____ protocol.
    A. Bluetooth   B. IP   C. TCP   D. UDP

22. A wireless router typically allows devices to connect to
    A. a wired network
    B. a wireless network
    C. both wired and wireless networks
    D. predefined devices on other networks

23. _____ may refer to a Wi-Fi use without permission.
    A. Piggybacking   B. Address breach
    C. Access point hack   D. IP address violation

24. FTTN in fiber networks denotes Fiber
    A. Technology Tracking Network
    B. to the Neighborhood
    C. Transmission Twisted Network
    D. Traceability Track Nationwide

25. PON stands for _____ Network.
    A. Passive Optic
    B. Private Optic
    C. Privately Owned
    D. Primary Operational

KEY (CORRECT ANSWERS)

1.	D		11.	A
2.	C		12.	C
3.	A		13.	A
4.	A		14.	C
5.	A		15.	A
6.	B		16.	A
7.	A		17.	B
8.	B		18.	A
9.	C		19.	A
10.	A		20.	D

21. A
22. C
23. A
24. B
25. A

TEST 3

DIRECTIONS: Each question or incomplete statement is followed by several suggested answers or completions. Select the one that BEST answers the question or completes the statement. *PRINT THE LETTER OF THE CORRECT ANSWER IN THE SPACE AT THE RIGHT.*

1. MIMO stands for
   A. Multiple Input Multiple Output
   B. Multiple Inter Modular Operations
   C. Metropolitan Inter Module Onset
   D. Metropolitan Intra Modular Offnet

   1.____

2. Beamforming characterizes
   A. merging of optic fiber streams
   B. merging of signals
   C. line of sight light beams
   D. unidirectional radio streams

   2.____

3. Speed of transmission will be SLOWEST in
   A. LAN   B. WAN   C. MAN   D. PAN

   3.____

4. Network Interface Cards (NIC) use a(n) _____ to distinguish one computer from another.
   A. network address
   B. IP address
   C. MAC address
   D. Checksum

   4.____

5. Which of the following amplify communication signals and filter noise?
   A. Hubs   B. Switches   C. Routers   D. Repeaters

   5.____

6. _____ send information/data to be copied unmodified to all computers.
   A. Hubs   B. Bridges   C. Firewalls   D. Switches

   6.____

7. Which of the following reject network access requests from unsafe sources?
   A. Filter services
   B. Hubs
   C. Security protocols
   D. Firewalls

   7.____

8. A _____ normally represents the smallest amount of data that can traverse over a network at a single time.
   A. byte   B. bit   C. word   D. packet

   8.____

9. OSPF is a
   A. routing protocol
   B. unique addressing scheme
   C. end user identification technique
   D. open source software

   9.____

10. _____ route is used when failure occurs with a routing device.
    A. Adaptive   B. Alternate   C. Access   D. Appropriate

    10.____

11. _____ is a parameter used for calculating a routing metric.
    A. Path speed   B. Load   C. Hop count   D. All of the above

    11.____

12. Algorithm in computer operations is a
    A. software B. hardware C. method D. pseudo code

13. _____ is the total time a packet takes to transmit from one place to another.
    A. Response time
    B. Latency
    C. Delay
    D. Bandwidth

14. Media portion in an OSI model includes
    A. presentation and data layer
    B. application and network layer
    C. transport and data layer
    D. all of the network data link and physical layers

15. OSI stands for Open
    A. Systems Interconnection
    B. Standards International
    C. Systems Integration
    D. Standards for Internet

16. Collision occurs when
    A. packets collide due to throttling
    B. more than one computer sends data at the same time
    C. data is sent out of sequence
    D. network traffic exceeds its limit

17. CSMA is a method used by
    A. Ethernet
    B. Internet
    C. operating system
    D. error detection services

18. The term broadband is used when a media type
    A. can carry multiple data signals
    B. can carry one signal at one time
    C. has separate lines for sending and receiving
    D. has error detection and correction mechanism

19. Fast Ethernet is also known as
    A. 10 Base-T
    B. 100 Base-T
    C. Gigabit Ethernet
    D. 1000 Base-X

20. _____ is called beacon frame.
    A. Periodically broadcasted frame
    B. Identification frame
    C. Header frame
    D. Frame beginning the broadcast

21. Channel bonding allows multiple _____ at the same time.
    A. packets B. channels C. media D. data streams

22. Gigabit Ethernet works on _____ media.
    A. fiber optic
    B. copper
    C. both fiber and copper
    D. wireless

23. FDDI uses _____ rings. 23.____
    A. four B. two C. one D. three

24. IPV6 addresses are _____ bits. 24.____
    A. 32 B. 65 C. 128 D. 256

25. IPV6 addresses are binary numbers represented in 25.____
    A. decimal B. binary C. octal D. hexadecimal

KEY (CORRECT ANSWERS)

1.	A	11.	D
2.	D	12.	C
3.	C	13.	B
4.	C	14.	D
5.	D	15.	A
6.	A	16.	B
7.	D	17.	A
8.	D	18.	A
9.	A	19.	B
10.	A	20.	A

21. B
22. C
23. B
24. C
25. D

TEST 4

DIRECTIONS: Each question or incomplete statement is followed by several suggested answers or completions. Select the one that BEST answers the question or completes the statement. *PRINT THE LETTER OF THE CORRECT ANSWER IN THE SPACE AT THE RIGHT.*

1. VoIP allows sending voice data using 1.____
   A. fiber optics B. PSTN
   C. standard IP D. copper wires

2. Bootstrapping refers to the _____ process. 2.____
   A. self-starting B. batch processing
   C. infinite D. automatically ending

3. NOS stands for Network 3.____
   A. Operation Starter B. On Standby
   C. Optic Stream D. Operating System

4. Compared to LANs, WANS are more 4.____
   A. reliable B. congested C. error-free D. cheaper

5. The initial setup costs for LAN are _____ compared to WAN. 5.____
   A. the same B. low C. high D. very high

6. WANs are often built using 6.____
   A. more than one adjacent LAN B. leased lines
   C. fiber optic cables D. extranet

7. The operating and maintenance costs of WAN are _____ compared to LAN. 7.____
   A. very low B. low C. high D. very high

8. Nowadays, most LAN(s) use _____ as standard. 8.____
   A. Ethernet B. VPN over Internet
   C. frame relay D. leased lines

9. WANs may use _____ as standard. 9.____
   A. Ethernet B. Subnet
   C. VPN D. Fast Ethernet

10. A computer network spanning three university campuses within remote geographical locations is a typical example of a _____ area network. 10.____
    A. campus B. wide C. metropolitan D. local

11. Client server networks require a _____ server. 11.____
    A. dedicated B. parallel C. data D. file

12. A file server will typically run _____ protocol. 12.____
    A. HTTP B. IP C. HTTPs D. FTP

47

13. _____ servers allow central administration of user and network resources.
    A. Print   B. Directory   C. File   D. Application

14. Network resources will be optimally used from a central resource in a _____ computer network model.
    A. central   B. distributed   C. remote   D. wireless

15. An internetwork will connect at least two
    A. internets   B. extranets   C. intranets   D. networks

16. Internet Protocol Security (IPSec) is a(n) _____ part of the IPV4.
    A. optional
    B. integral/mandatory
    C. built-in
    D. missing

17. Features of _____ can be extended by adding headers.
    A. IPV4   B. IPV6   C. IP   D. TCP

18. The available types of communication in IPV4 are unicast, multicast and
    A. podcast   B. broadcast   C. lancast   D. delicast

19. In backup terminology, a cold site means
    A. needs time to switch to normal operations
    B. readily available backup
    C. a backup on Cloud
    D. a separate backup

20. An overlapping frame is called a(n)
    A. header
    B. packet
    C. collision
    D. extended frame

21. _____ is a set of checks/rules for communication.
    A. Protocol
    B. Syntax
    C. Lexical grammar
    D. Encryption

22. Multiplexing collects data from different
    A. networks   B. applications   C. addresses   D. routers

23. When a block of data is transmitted, supplement data is attached to the _____ for use from one layer to another.
    A. datagram   B. packet   C. FIN bit   D. header

24. De-multiplexing is done in a(n) _____ layer.
    A. transport   B. network   C. data   D. application

25. In large networks, a _____ will divide the network into logical parts called segments to handle data traffic.
    A. switch   B. hub   C. router   D. bridge

KEY (CORRECT ANSWERS)

1.	C	11.	A
2.	A	12.	D
3.	D	13.	C
4.	B	14.	A
5.	B	15.	D
6.	B	16.	B
7.	C	17.	B
8.	A	18.	B
9.	C	19.	A
10.	C	20.	C

21.	A
22.	B
23.	D
24.	A
25.	C

EXAMINATION SECTION
TEST 1

DIRECTIONS: Each question or incomplete statement is followed by several suggested answers or completions. Select the one that BEST answers the question or completes the statement. *PRINT THE LETTER OF THE CORRECT ANSWER IN THE SPACE AT THE RIGHT.*

1. Modern day telephony uses _____ for sending voice signals. 1._____
   A. VoIP B. modems C. routers D. switches

2. A user is downloading a file using a computer on the network. The computer is a(n) 2._____
   A. node B. entry point C. client D. access point

3. A network operating system offers its services to 3._____
   A. groups of computers using desktop operating system
   B. groups of servers connected to LAN
   C. users in another network segment
   D. all of the above

4. The program to interpret HTML files sent from a web server is called 4._____
   A. browser B. SMTP server
   C. RAS D. HTML engine

5. FrameRelay is used in 5._____
   A. LAN B. MAN C. WAN D. PAN

6. The most secure network is 6._____
   A. LAN B. MAN C. WAN D. PAN

7. In a _____ network, any computer could be a client or server. 7._____
   A. peer-to-peer B. client server
   B. VLAN D. terrestrial

8. User documents have been stored on a central server for printing. This is an example of a(n) _____ server. 8._____
   A. application B. file C. print D. mail

9. Small computer programs are being run from a central computer. This is a(n) _____ kind of server. 9._____
   A. application B. file c. print D. mail

10. Databases are stored in a(n) _____ server. 10._____
    A. database B. file C. data D. information

11. Data resources are placed at different geographical locations, however, they are managed from one unique location. What kind of network model is this? 11._____
    A. Centralized B. Remote C. Distributed D. Isolated

51

12. A company has a private network used within its premises. It has given access to a few outside suppliers through its
    A. intranet   B. extranet   C. internet   D. subnet

13. You are using your browser to browse a web page using HTTP protocol. _____ protocol will be used to respond to your request.
    A. HTTP   B. TCP   C. HTTPS   D. IP

14. _____ protocols are not specific to one supplier of LAN equipment.
    A. Proprietary   B. Functional   C. Universal   D. Standard

15. RFCs are used to upgrade the bandwidth requirements of a protocol. RFC stands for
    A. Requirement for Formal Consent   B. Regional Formats Committee
    C. Request For Comments   D. Released Future Concerns

16. LAN standards for networking are developed by _____ organization.
    A. IERT   B. IEEE   C. FERS   D. OOEE

17. Standard allocation of Internet protocol addresses are insured by an organization called
    A. ICANN   B. Internet Architecture Board (IAB)
    C. IEEE   D. Internet Society

18. A network switch is connected to 15 employees. _____ topology is in use.
    A. Star   B. Bus   C. Ring   D. Hybrid

19. _____ optic fiber cable will be used for smaller distances.
    A. Single Mode Fiber (SMF)   B. Multi-Mode Fiber (MMF)
    C. Both A and B   D. None of the above

20. The entire bandwidth of a digital signal is being used by the only channel. It is called a(n) _____ communication.
    A. broadband   B. digital   C. analog   D. baseband

21. Frequency Division Multiplexing (FDM) is possible in
    A. baseband   B. broadband
    C. both A and B   D. none of the above

22. Gigabit Ethernet is capable of transmissions of 1000
    A. BPS   B. GBPS   C. MBPS   D. KBPS

23. Fiber distributed data interface uses _____ topology.
    A. ring   B. star   C. mesh   D. bus

24. IEEE networking standards apply to the _____ layer specifications technology.
    A. network   B. data   C. application   D. physical

25. Mutual authentication between the client and the server is called 25.____
    A. encrypted
    B. decrypted
    C. challenge handshake
    D. kerberos

KEY (CORRECT ANSWERS)

1.	A		11.	C
2.	C		12.	B
3.	D		13.	A
4.	A		14.	D
5.	C		15.	C
6.	A		16.	B
7.	A		17.	A
8.	B		18.	A
9.	A		19.	A
10.	A		20.	D

21. B
22. C
23. A
24. A
25. A

EXAMINATION SECTION
TEST 1

DIRECTIONS: Each question or incomplete statement is followed by several suggested answers or completions. Select the one that BEST answers the question or completes the statement. *PRINT THE LETTER OF THE CORRECT ANSWER IN THE SPACE AT THE RIGHT.*

1. A voice grade line is a line which

    A. is directly connected from point to point
    B. has a speed of 600-4800 bits per second
    C. is used for voice transmission only
    D. does not have signaling capability

    1._____

2. A half-duplex line is one which

    A. transmits in one direction only
    B. transmits in both directions simultaneously
    C. requires four wires for transmission
    D. transmits in both directions, but only in one direction at a time

    2._____

3. The CHIEF advantage of a switched line as compared to a private line is that a switched line has

    A. low cost if the line has low usage
    B. higher line capacity
    C. ability to compensate for distortion
    D. greater signal-to-noise ratio

    3._____

4. A telephone line of 3000 hz. bandwidth with a signal-to-noise ratio of 20 db. has a *theoretical maximum* capacity of

    A. 17, 300 bits per second
    B. 19, 900 bits per second
    C. 23, 100 bits per second
    D. 27, 600 bits per second

    4._____

5. A conditioned line is defined as one which

    A. is available in a switched network
    B. is used only on a part-time basis
    C. has rigid specifications on amplitude variation and envelope delay
    D. is available as a simplex line

    5._____

6. A factor that distinguishes a coaxial cable line from wire pairs is that a coaxial cable line has

    A. a smaller bandwidth than wire pairs
    B. more crosstalk between cables than wire pairs
    C. lower propagation speeds than wire pairs
    D. less delay distortion than wire pairs

    6._____

7. A microwave relay line does NOT

    A. require fewer amplifiers per mile than a coaxial line

    7._____

B. require a line of sight path
C. react to adverse weather conditions
D. cost more per mile than comparable coaxial line

8. In the absence of any noise, a telegraph type line of 300 hz. bandwidth with two voltage sending levels is *theoretically* capable of transmitting

    A. 600 bits per second
    B. 300 bits per second
    C. 150 bits per second
    D. 75 bits per second

9. The speed of a transmission line is often quoted as being a certain number of "bauds." If the line can be in any of four possible states at any given time, the number of bits per second transmitted will be

    A. equal to the number of "bauds"
    B. twice the number of "bauds"
    C. half the number of "bauds"
    D. four times the number of "bauds"

10. If a rectangular pulse is passed through a band limited line (0-3000 hz), the output of the line will have

    A. the vertical sides of the pulse with finite slope
    B. the flat top of the pulse tilted
    C. both the flat top of the pulse tilted and the vertical sides of the pulse with finite slope
    D. no distortion in the pulse

11. "Systematic Distortion" is defined as distortion which

    A. is produced from input to output
    B. can be predicted and thus compensated for
    C. is characteristic only of a single component of the system
    D. can include noise and switch chatter as one of its components

12. Distortion on a line due to a non-linear phase shift with frequency is

    A. *unimportant* for voice transmission, since understanding of speech is unaffected by it
    B. *unimportant* for data transmission, since only rms values of voltage are detected
    C. *necessary* for proper voice and data transmission
    D. *necessary* only for proper voice transmission

13. "Gaussian" noise is noise which

    A. is caused by magnetic circuits
    B. varies about a signal level in a purely random fashion
    C. is caused by rhythmic phenomena
    D. is caused by lightning

14. "White" noise is NOT noise which

    A. on the average contains all spectral frequencies equally
    B. is due to thermal effects

C. can be eliminated by cooling equipment to absolute zero
D. is caused by switch chatter

15. If the bandwidth of a system is increased, the noise power generated in an electrical conductor will   15.____

    A. increase proportionately with the bandwidth
    B. decrease inversely with the bandwidth
    C. be unaffected by the bandwidth
    D. vary only slightly with the bandwidth

Questions 16-18.

DIRECTIONS: For Questions 16 through 18 inclusive, reference should be made to the following generalized expression for a modulated signal: $a_c = A_c \sin(2\pi f_c t + \theta_c)$

16. If the signal information is contained as part of the A_c term, the modulation is called   16.____

    A. amplitude modulation
    B. frequency modulation
    C. phase modulation
    D. pulse code modulation

17. If the signal is contained in the θ_c term, the modulation is called   17.____

    A. amplitude modulation
    B. frequency modulation
    C. phase modulation
    D. pulse code modulation

18. If the signal is contained in the f_c term, the modulation is called   18.____

    A. amplitude modulation
    B. frequency modulation
    C. phase modulation
    D. pulse code modulation

19. If the pulse train shown below is modulating a sine wave carrier and the result is as shown below, then the modulation is   19.____

    A. amplitude modulation
    B. frequency modulation
    C. phase modulation
    D. pulse code modulation

20. If the pulse train shown below is modulating a sine wave carrier and the result is as shown below, then the modulation is   20.____

A. amplitude modulation
C. phase modulation
B. frequency modulation
D. pulse code modulation

21. If a carrier of 60,000 hz is amplitude modulated by a 1500 hz sine wave, the modulated signal will contain frequencies only of

    A. 60,000 and 1500 hz
    B. 60,000 and 61,500 hz
    C. 60,000, 61,500 and 58,500 hz
    D. 61,500 and 58,500 hz

21.____

22. The modulation index of an AM signal is defined as the

    A. relative power of the carrier
    B. relative power of the modulating signal
    C. ratio of the modulation amplitude to the carrier amplitude
    D. absolute power of the total signal

22.____

23. If the value of the modulation index were to exceed unity in an AM system, the

    A. modulation would be more efficient
    B. carrier wave's amplitude would be less than the modulating wave's amplitude
    C. signal could not be recovered without distortion
    D. transmitter would pulse on and off

23.____

24. If the modulating signal is not sinusoidal in an AM system, the one of the following results which is MOST likely to occur is that

    A. the output will be distorted
    B. a band of frequencies will be generated rather than a single set of sidebands
    C. the frequency of the carrier will shift
    D. linear analysis will not apply

24.____

25. The one of the following statements which is *true* of single sideband amplitude modulation is that it *usually*

    A. requires greater bandwidth than full AM
    B. improves the signal-to-noise ratio over full AM
    C. loses information content
    D. requires greater transmitting power than full AM

25.____

26. Envelope detection of an AM signal will

    A. not require a reference signal
    B. not require both sidebands
    C. be more expensive than "synchronous detection"
    D. require less bandwidth than "synchronous detection"

26.____

27. "Synchronous, coherent, or homodyne" detection of an AM signal will

    A. not require a reference signal
    B. not require filtering

27.____

C. be less expensive than envelope detection
D. require less bandwidth than envelope detection

28. When a sine wave is frequency modulated by a low frequency sine wave, 28.____

    A. only three sidebands are generated
    B. the number of sidebands depends on the modulating frequency
    C. the carrier is suppressed
    D. an infinite number of sidebands is theoretically generated

29. If a pulse signal is used to modulate a carrier, the 29.____

    A. carrier can only be amplitude modulated
    B. carrier can only be frequency modulated
    C. modulation to be chosen depends on the particular code
    D. carrier can be either amplitude modulated or frequency modulated

30. Of the following, the maximum sampling interval which permits complete reconstruction of a band-limited signal in the range 0-3,000 hz is, *most nearly,* 30.____

    A. 0.1 milliseconds   B. 0.3 milliseconds
    C. 1.0 milliseconds   D. 10.0 milliseconds

KEYS (CORRECT ANSWERS)

1.	B	16.	A
2.	D	17.	C
3.	A	18.	B
4.	B	19.	A
5.	C	20.	B
6.	D	21.	C
7.	D	22.	C
8.	A	23.	C
9.	B	24.	B
10.	A	25.	B
11.	B	26.	A
12.	A	27.	D
13.	B	28.	D
14.	D	29.	D
15.	A	30.	A

TEST 2

DIRECTIONS: Each question or incomplete statement is followed by several suggested answers or completions. Select the one that BEST answers the question or completes the statement. *PRINT THE LETTER OF THE CORRECT ANSWER IN THE SPACE AT THE RIGHT.*

1. The MAIN disadvantage of pulse code transmission as compared to analog transmission is that in pulse code transmission   1.___

    A. the signal-to-noise ratio is low
    B. repeater stations add noise to the system
    C. a greater bandwidth is required
    D. it is more expensive than frequency division multi plexing

2. In a pulse amplitude modulation system, the analog signal is converted to a series of pulses which   2.___

    A. are unequally spaced according to the analog signal amplitude
    B. start at equal time increments but are of unequal duration according to the amplitude of the analog signal
    C. are of equal spacing and duration but whose amplitude varies with the analog signal
    D. are of equal duration but whose spacing depends on the analog signal

3. In a pulse duration (width) modulation system, the analog signal is converted to a series of pulses which   3.___

    A. start at equal time increments but whose durations are proportional to the amplitude of the analog signal
    B. are unequally spaced in time in accordance with the amplitude of the analog signal
    C. are of equal spacing and duration but whose amplitude varies with the analog signal
    D. are of equal duration but whose spacing depends on the analog frequency

4. Before an analog signal can be sent by pulse code modulation it must be quantized. This means that the   4.___

    A. frequency must be determined
    B. zero crossings must be counted
    C. signal must be passed through a band pass filter
    D. analog values must be selected so that they fall into discrete values

5. When an analog signal to be sent by pulse code modulation is quantized and sampled, the result that is transmitted is a   5.___

    A. pulse of amplitude approximately equal to the amplitude of the analog signal
    B. pulse of duration approximately proportional to the amplitude of the analog signal
    C. series of pulses equal to a binary representation of the amplitude of the sampled signal
    D. sequence of pulses generated at the zero crossings of the analog signal

6. When several different signals are sent on a single cable by modulating several different carriers, the process is known as

   A. time division multiplexing
   B. time slice multiplexing
   C. single sideband transmission
   D. frequency division multiplexing

   6._____

7. Space division multiplexing involves

   A. several signals at different center frequencies in a cable
   B. sampled signals sent in a time sequential manner
   C. several coaxial units grouped into a single cable
   D. multiplexing of signals by microwaves

   7._____

8. When signals are multiplexed using frequency division multiplexing, they are usually passed through a low pass filter first. This is done PRIMARILY because

   A. higher frequencies need more power
   B. low frequencies have more power
   C. the filters cannot be ideal
   D. it prevents crosstalk between channels

   8._____

9. "Guard Bands" in a frequency division multiplexer are necessary MAINLY because

   A. better use can be made of the available bandwidth
   B. filters cannot have infinitely steep sides
   C. carrier frequencies must be identified
   D. the sidebands are equal

   9._____

10. The MAIN disadvantage of frequency division multiplexing as compared with time division multiplexing is that

    A. less efficient use is made of the band
    B. with current technology the expense of building filters is greater than the expense of building logic circuits
    C. signals cannot be continuous
    D. the transmission quality is lower

    10._____

11. In a time division multiplexing system,

    A. complete messages are transmitted over frequency bands that are separated from each other
    B. several messages are sampled and the samples are transmitted sequentially
    C. complete messages are transmitted sequentially
    D. sampled messages are transmitted over "guarded" frequency bands

    11._____

12. A time division multiplexed system

    A. requires a means of accurately synchronizing transmitter and receiver
    B. allows samples to be packed tightly together
    C. cannot be used with binary coding
    D. cannot be used to transmit computer data

    12._____

13. A Time Assignment Speech Interpolation (TASI) system is one which

    A. completes messages before transmitting them
    B. combines time division multiplexing and frequency division multiplexing
    C. is a method of pulse position modulation for speech
    D. is useful for transmission of large amounts of continuous data

14. Pulse code modulation is to be used to transmit an analog signal below 3000 hz. Each sample is coded at one of 64 levels.
    Of the following, the number of bits per second that must be transmitted is, *most nearly,*

    A. 3000   B. 6000   C. 18,000   D. 36,000

15. In order to decrease the bandwidth needed for pulse code modulation, one should

    A. *increase* the number of quantizing levels
    B. *decrease* the number of quantizing levels
    C. *increase* the bandwidth of the modulating signal
    D. *decrease* the sampling time

16. Of the following, the MAIN purpose of a "modem" or "data set" in a computer-terminal system is to

    A. provide an interface between the terminal and the computer
    B. convert terminal (computer) signals to modulated signals for transmission by common carrier and vice versa
    C. standardize codes
    D. provide the means for voice communication on a data line

17. The one of the following which is a *correct* statement regarding modems or "data sets" is that they

    A. are necessary on all terminal-computer combinations
    B. are necessary if communication lines are frequency multiplexed
    C. do not improve the speed of transmission
    D. must be used only if the distance between terminal and computer is greater than 150 feet

18. In order to convert an analog signal to a digital signal,

    A. the signal first must be differentiated
    B. the signal first must be integrated
    C. a precise reference level is necessary
    D. a clock pulse must be accumulated

19. One scheme for analog-to-digital conversion is shown below:

    The CHIEF asset of such a scheme is

A. high speed   B. accuracy
C. low cost   D. high sampling rate

20. The HIGHEST rate of analog-to-digital conversion consistent with the present level of technology is, *most nearly,*

    A. 200 /sec   B. 50,000 /sec   C. 10^6 /sec   D. 10^9 /sec

21. A three-bit binary parallel signal is to be converted to an analog signal by means of the following circuit:

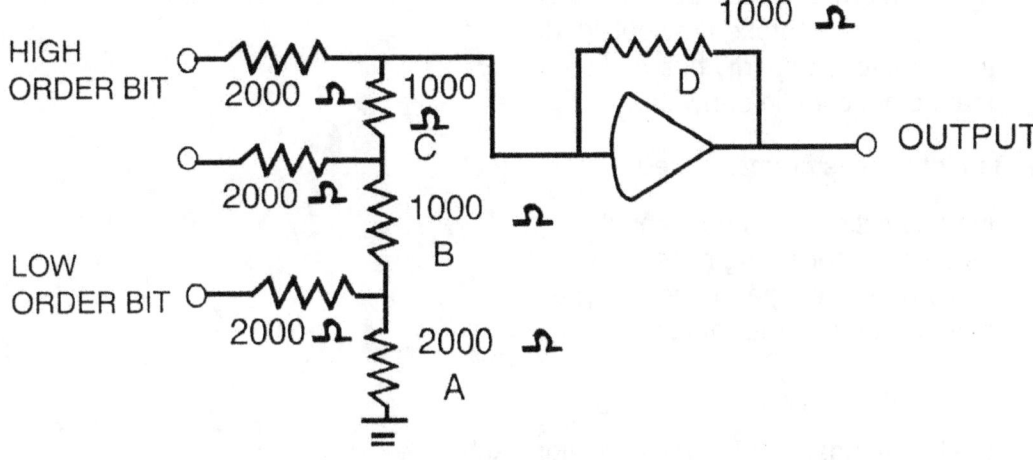

    In this circuit the resistor whose accuracy is of LEAST importance is

    A. A   B. B   C. C   D. D

22. A three-bit binary parallel signal is to be converted to an analog signal by means of the following circuit:

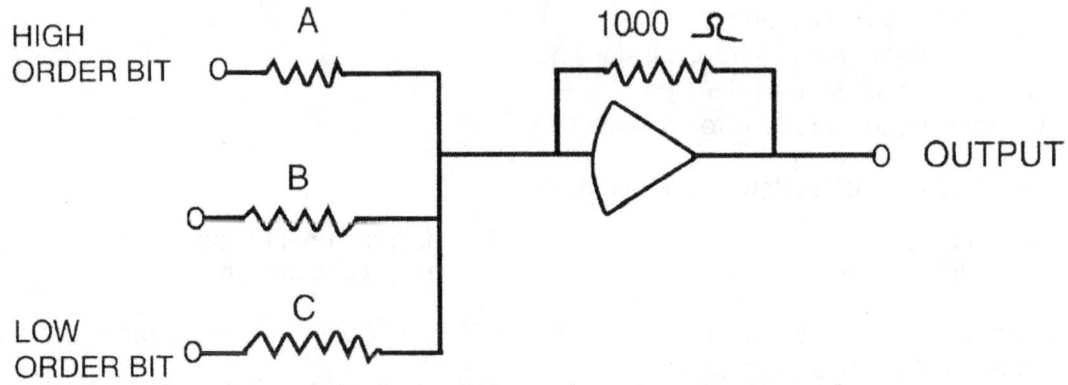

    In this circuit, resistors A, B, C should have the values, in ohms, of

    A. A=1000 B=500 C=250   B. A=250 B=500 C=1000
    C. A=1000 B=100 C=1000   D. A=1000 B=2000 C=3000

23. In order to convert a serial binary number into an analog signal,

    A. bits must not be sampled
    B. only the most significant bit can be used
    C. serial bits must be stored in a shift register and presented in parallel
    D. analog signals must be converted to DC

24. Of the following, the type of error MOST likely to occur in a process involving conversion from analog-to-digital and then back to analog, is

    A. noise in the transmission system
    B. phase delay
    C. frequency distortion
    D. quantization distortion

25. "Error correcting codes" are codes

    A. whose information can be retrieved even though some bits are lost
    B. that cannot be "broken" by outsiders
    C. that contain odd parity bits
    D. that do not contain parity bits

26. The Baudot code is *normally* used

    A. in transmitting between computers
    B. as an error correcting code
    C. as a code in telegraph and teletype
    D. only on computer terminals

27. The ASCII code is

    A. the US standard code for information exchange
    B. the only code permitted as computer input
    C. limited to computer use
    D. a six-bit code

28. A parity bit in a code is

    A. a bit added to an array of bits to insure that the sum of all the bits is either always odd or always even
    B. never sent along a transmission line
    C. sent or not sent as directed
    D. only used for local error checking

29. The AT&T #33 ASR teletype operates using the

    A. Baudot code   B. five-channel teletype code
    C. ASCII code   D. parity checking feature

30. In order to send the sequence of characters A3C2 in ASCII code, the *number* of 7 bit characters that must be sent is

    A. 8   B. 7   C. 6   D. 4

KEYS (CORRECT ANSWERS)

1.	C		16.	B
2.	C		17.	B
3.	A		18.	C
4.	D		19.	C
5.	C		20.	C
6.	D		21.	A
7.	C		22.	B
8.	D		23.	C
9.	B		24.	D
10.	B		25.	A
11.	B		26.	C
12.	A		27.	A
13.	B		28.	A
14.	D		29.	C
15.	B		30.	D

TEST 3

DIRECTIONS: Each question or incomplete statement is followed by several suggested answers or completions. Select the one that BEST answers the question or completes the statement. *PRINT THE LETTER OF THE CORRECT ANSWER IN THE SPACE AT THE RIGHT.*

1. The CHIEF asset of a magnetic core memory system is the

    A. low cost of the system
    B. quantity of data that can be stored
    C. speed with which a fetch or a store of data can be executed
    D. volatility of the storage

2. The disc storage memory unit is used PRIMARILY when

    A. large amounts of data must be accessed randomly and fairly fast
    B. the expense of storage is the chief concern
    C. data must be accessed rapidly and very often
    D. long term storage is needed with only occasional access

3. When data is stored on magnetic tape, it is normally "blocked." This means

    A. the tape cannot be erased
    B. a large amount of data is recorded between unrecorded gaps
    C. the tape cannot be written over
    D. the data items are individually accessible

4. In a multiterminal computer system, terminals are "polled" sequentially. This means that

    A. each terminal is connected for its own "time slot"
    B. each terminal transmits when ready
    C. a signal is sent inquiring if a particular terminal is ready to transmit
    D. terminals "seize" the input on an interrupt basis

5. Terminal devices can operate in different codes. The means of conversion from one code to another which is MOST efficient *timewise* is

    A. hardware   B. memory table
    C. program manipulation   D. commutation

6. The number 15 (decimal) is equivalent to the binary number

    A. 1111   B. 1050   C. 1010   D. 0017

7. The number 10110 (binary) is equivalent to the decimal number,

    A. 111   B. 22   C. 26   D. 19

8. The number 110101 (binary) is equivalent to the octal number,

    A. 53   B. 37   C. 46   D. 65

9. The number 73 (octal) is equivalent to the binary number,

    A. 101101   B. 59   C. 111011   D. 55

10. The number 27 (decimal) is equivalent to the octal number,   10._____

    A. 17   B. 10111   C. 11011   D. 33

11. The following is a list of current addresses and locations to be addressed, in a DEC PDP/   11._____
    8 computer:

	Current addresses	Location to be addressed
1.	0050	0120
2.	1230	1377
3.	2742	2450
4.	6555	6600

    Of the following statements pertaining to this list, the one which is *correct* is that

    A. all the second locations must be addressed directly
    B. all the second locations must be addressed indirectly
    C. the second locations for 1 and 2 can be addressed directly and for 3 and 4 must be addressed indirectly
    D. the second location for 1 and 4 must be addressed directly and for 2 and 3 must be addressed indirectly

12. The following is a DEC PDP/8 program: 12._____
    ```
    *200
           START,    CLA CLL
                     TAD A
                     CIA
                     DCA TALLY
           MULT,     TAD B
                     ISZ TALLY
                     JMP MULT
                     HLT
           A,        0022
           B,        0044
           TALLY,    0000
    $
    ```
    When the program stops, the one of the following which will be stored in location B is

    A. 0022_8 B. 1210_8 C. 0044_8 D. 648_8

13. The following is a DEC PDP/8 program: 13._____
    ```
    *200
           START,    CLA CLL
                     TAD COUNT
                     CIA
                     DCA TALLY
           ADD,      TAD 300
                     ISZ ADD
                     ISZ TALLY
                     JMP ADD
    ```

```
                        DCA SUM
                        HLT
            COUNT,      0100
            TALLY,      0000
            SUM,        0000
        $
```
This program sums 100_8 numbers in locations

- A. 100_8 to 177_8 and stores the sum in the location SUM
- B. 100_8 to 177_8 and displays the sum in the accumulator
- C. 300_8 to 377_8 and stores the sum in the location SUM
- D. 300_8 to 377_8 and displays the sum in the accumulator

14. The following is a DEC PDP/8 program:

```
        *200
            TEST,       CLA CLL
                        TAD B
                        CIA
                        TAD A
                        SMA CLA
                        HLT
                        TAD A
                        DCA TEMP
                        TAD B
                        DCA A
                        TAD TEMP
                        DCA B
                        HLT
            A,          1234
            B,          2460
            TEMP,
        $
```

At the end of program execution, the content of location

- A. A and location B are the same
- B. A is larger than that of location B
- C. A is smaller than that of location B
- D. A is zero

15. The following is an incomplete DEC PDP/8 program to print one ASCII character stored in a memory location:

```
        *200
            START,      CLA CLL
                        TLS
                        TAD HOLD
                        missing instruction
                        HLT
            TYPE,       0
                        TSF
```

4 (#3)

```
            JMP,-1
            TLS
            CLA CLL
            JMP I TYPE
HOLD,       301
$
```

The instruction missing from this program is

A. JMP TYPE B. JMS TYPE C. SKP D. SPA

16. In FORTRAN, the statement involving "WRITE" in conjunction with the FORMAT statement will

    A. control the input of the data
    B. control the way data is stored in memory
    C. alter the form of stored numbers
    D. control the manner in which output is printed

16._____

17. A portion of a FORTRAN program is shown below:
```
A=6.0
B=4.0
C=2.0
E=3.0
D=A + B/C + E
```
The result stored in D after these steps, will be

A. 2.0 B. 11.0 C. 6.8 D. 8.0

17._____

18. A portion of a FORTRAN program is shown below:
```
C=6.0
D=2.0
E=2.0
F=1.0
A=C/D**E*(F + 1.0)
```
The result stored in A after these steps, will be

A. 0.75 B. 3.0 C. 0.375 D. 18.0

18._____

19. A portion of a FORTRAN program is shown below:
```
        M=0
8       DO 17,N=1, 3
17      M=M+N
        K=M
```
The result stored in K after these steps, will be

A. 1 B. 3 C. 6 D. 10

19._____

20. A portion of a FORTRAN program is shown below:
```
        T=-3.0
15      IF(T)10,20,30
10      S=5.0
        GO TO 50
20      S=10.0
```

20._____

69

```
            GO TO 50
    30      S=15.0
    50      V=S
```
The result stored in V after these steps, will be

A. 5.0   B. -3.0   C. 10.0   D. 15.0

21. The time average of a measured quantity can be *approximated* by

    A. sampling more than twice per cycle
    B. differentiating and sampling more than twice per cycle
    C. integrating for a fixed length of time
    D. integrating for a variable length of time

22. When a signal tends to be "noisy," the effect of integrating the signal will be to

    A. accentuate the high frequency noise
    B. eliminate the high frequency noise
    C. increase the effective bandwidth of the system
    D. make the output respond more readily to fast input changes

23. Integrators, unless carefully designed and constructed, have a tendency to

    A. reduce the gain of the system
    B. be noisy
    C. have their DC level drift
    D. stretch the frequency band

24. For telemetry purposes, high level radioactivity can be measured BEST by means of a(n)

    A. electroscope   B. manometer
    C. film gauge   D. geiger counter

25. Sulfur dioxide content in an air sample can be measured BEST by passing

    A. the air through water and measuring the conductivity change
    B. ultraviolet light through the air sample and measuring the diffraction
    C. infrared light through the air sample and measuring the absorption
    D. the air sample through a filter paper and measuring the change in reflectance

26. Carbon monoxide content in an air sample can be measured BEST by passing

    A. the air through water and measuring the conductivity change
    B. ultraviolet light through the air sample and measuring the diffraction
    C. infrared light through the sample and measuring the absorption
    D. the air sample through a filter paper and measuring the change in reflectance

27. "Smoke shade" information for air pollution monitoring is obtained by passing

    A. the air through water and measuring the conductivity change
    B. ultraviolet light through the sample and measuring the diffraction
    C. infrared light through the sample and measuring the absorption
    D. the air sample through a filter paper and measuring the change in reflectance

28. Wind direction can be telemetered by data from a

   A. manoscope connected to a weathervane
   B. wind vane connected to a synchro system
   C. wind vane connected to a hygrometer
   D. propeller connected to a magneto

29. Wind speed can BEST be telemetered by data from a

   A. pitot tube
   B. manometer
   C. propeller-driven magneto
   D. evaporative cooling effect

30. Of the following, the BEST description of a telemetered sensor for temperature measurement is a

   A. conductivity change of water measured by a conductance cell
   B. temperature sensitive resistor measured by an ohmmeter
   C. temperature sensitive resistor measured by a selfbalancing Wheatstone bridge
   D. frequency shift oscillator

KEYS (CORRECT ANSWERS)

1.	C	16.	D
2.	A	17.	B
3.	B	18.	B
4.	C	19.	C
5.	A	20.	A
6.	A	21.	C
7.	B	22.	B
8.	D	23.	C
9.	C	24.	D
10.	D	25.	A
11.	C	26.	C
12.	C	27.	D
13.	C	28.	B
14.	B	29.	C
15.	B	30.	C

TEST 4

DIRECTIONS: Each question or incomplete statement is followed by several suggested answers or completions. Select the one that BEST answers the question or completes the statement. *PRINT THE LETTER OF THE CORRECT ANSWER IN THE SPACE AT THE RIGHT.*

1. Assuming the velocity of light to be 3×10^8 meters per second, the frequency of electromagnetic energy having a wave length of 1×10^{-5} centimeters, is (in cycles per second)

    A. 3×10^5 B. 1×10^{13} C. 1×10^{14} D. 3×10^{15}

    1.____

2. Two metal spheres are suspended by insulating threads so that they are touching. A charged body is then brought NEAR one of the spheres and away from the other and held there while the spheres are moved apart. After the rod is removed, the spheres will

    A. *repel each other* because of equal negative charges on each
    B. *repel each other* because of equal positive charges on each
    C. *attract each other* because opposite charges were induced on each
    D. *have no mutual electrostatic effect* because no charge was transferred

    2.____

3. Of the following, when an atom emits an alpha particle, its MASS NUMBER is

    A. *decreased* by 4 and its ATOMIC NUMBER is *increased* by 2
    B. *increased* by 4 and its ATOMIC NUMBER is *decreased* by 2
    C. *increased* by 4 and its ATOMIC NUMBER is *increased* by 2
    D. *decreased* by 4 and its ATOMIC NUMBER is *decreased* by 2

    3.____

4. The Doppler effect is associated *most closely* with that property of sound or light known as

    A. amplitude   B. velocity   C. frequency   D. intensity

    4.____

5. Of the following, the TRUE statement about X-rays is that they are

    A. electromagnetic rays having a smaller wave length than gamma rays
    B. longitudinal waves having a frequency range above 12,000 v.p.s.
    C. transverse waves having a smaller wave length than ultra violet waves
    D. transverse waves having a wave length range of 4000 to 8000 Angstroms

    5.____

6. Which *one* of the following is a CHARACTERISTIC of a parallel electrical circuit?

    A. The current is the same in all parts of the circuit.
    B. The voltage across all the branches is the same.
    C. A break through any part of the circuit will stop the flow of current throughout the circuit.
    D. The total resistance is equal to the sum of the resistances of the component parts.

    6.____

7. Quasi-stellar radio sources have been found which radiate energy at the rate of 10^{44} ergs per second. This power, when converted into watts, is CLOSEST to which one of the following?

    A. 10^6 B. 10^7 C. 10^{37} D. 10^{51}

    7.____

8. If the molecules in a cylinder of oxygen and those in a cylinder of hydrogen have the *same* average speed, *then*

    A. both gases have the *same* temperature
    B. both gases have the *same* pressure
    C. the hydrogen has the *higher* temperature
    D. the oxygen has the *higher* temperature

9. Just as the photon is a *quantum* in electromagnetic field theory, *which one* of the following is considered to be the *quantum* in the nuclear field?

    A. Neutrino   B. Electron   C. Meson   D. Neutron

10. When an electron moves with a speed equal to 4/5 that of light, the *ratio* of the mass to its rest mass is

    A. 5/4   B. 5/3   C. 25/9   D. 25/16

11. When accelerating a proton, a synchrotron subjects the proton to an electric field whose frequency

    A. *varies, and* to a *varying* magnetic field intensity
    B. *varies, and* to a *constant* magnetic field intensity
    C. *is constant,* and to a *constant* magnetic field intensity
    D. *is constant,* and to a *varying* magnetic field intensity

12. Under optimum conditions of irradiation, photoelectrons of HIGHEST energy will be ejected by *which one* of the following?

    A. Ultraviolet radiation   B. Infrared radiation
    C. Monochromatic yellow light   D. Gamma rays

13. Assume that a particle is moving at a speed near that of light. In order to halve its Einstein energy equivalence, the particle's speed must be *reduced*

    A. to of its original value
    B. to $\frac{1}{4}$ of its original value
    C. to of its original value
    D. until its relativistic mass is halved

14. The frequency of a wave motion is doubled while the amplitude is held constant. The intensity of the wave motion *now* will be

    A. the same as that of the former wave motion
    B. multiplied by 2
    C. divided by 2
    D. multiplied by 4

15. Three ideal components -- a resistor, an inductor, and a capacitor - are connected in series to a source of a-c. The potential difference across each component is 40 volts. The *total voltage* across the three components is

    A. zero   B. $40\sqrt{2}$v   C. 40v   D. 120v

16. The potential difference across a 6-ohm resistor is 6 volts. The *power* used by the resistor is, in watts,

    A. 6 B. 12 C. 18 D. 24

17. Of the following, the *one* that is NOT normally used as a component of some electronic oscillator circuits is the

    A. lighthouse tube B. pitot tube
    C. klystron D. magnetron

18. If a charged capacitor loses one-half its charge by leakage, it has lost what fraction of its store of energy?

    A. 1/8 B. 1/4 C. 1/2 D. 3/4

19. The force, in newtons, required to stop a bullet that has a mass of 15g and a velocity of 400 m/sec in a distance of 20 cm, will be

    A. 4,000 B. 5,000 C. 6,000 D. 8,000

20. Of the following, the *unit* that is NOT used to measure the torque of a rotating body is

    A. lb-ft B. m-newton C. slug-ft D. cm-dyne

21. A 2 lb body vibrates in simple harmonic motion with an amplitude of 3 in and a period of 5 sec. The acceleration at the mid-point will be, in in/sec, CLOSEST to *which one* of the following?

    A. 0 B. 0.6 C. 1.2 D. 3.8

22. In connection with the molecular theory of matter, which one of the following is NOT assumed to be *accurate*?

    A. Effects of individual molecules are easily observed
    B. Law of conservation of kinetic energy
    C. Newton's laws of motion
    D. Law of conservation of momentum

23. Of the following, the force which to the LEAST extent follows an inverse-square law is

    A. electrical B. nuclear C. magnetic D. gravitational

24. In a nuclear pile, boron rods are used for

    A. fuel B. shielding C. control D. moderation

25. Antimatter consists of atoms containing

    A. protons, neutrons, and electrons
    B. protons, meutrons, and positrons
    C. antiprotons, antineutrons, and positrons
    D. antiprotons, antineutrons, and electrons

26. A high-energy gamma ray may materialize into a(n)

    A. meson B. electron and a proton
    C. proton and a neutron D. electron and a positron

27. The usefulness of the early cyclotron was LIMITED by the fact that 27.____
    A. the supply of electrical power was limited
    B. magnetic fields could not be sufficiently increased
    C. the mass of electrons increases at high velocities
    D. it was too expensive

28. The Wimshurst Machine is used to study 28.____
    A. electrostatic charges   B. radioactivity
    C. electrolysis   D. the electric motor

29. Light can be polarized by the use of 29.____
    A. an electric current through a wire
    B. a calcite crystal
    C. powerful magnets
    D. an electrostatic field

30. If $_{84}Po^{210}$ emits a beta particle, the resulting nucleus will have an atomic number of 30.____
    A. 82   B. 83   C. 84   D. 85

KEYS (CORRECT ANSWERS)

1.	D	16.	A
2.	C	17.	B
3.	D	18.	D
4.	C	19.	C
5.	C	20.	C
6.	B	21.	A
7.	C	22.	A
8.	D	23.	B
9.	C	24.	C
10.	B	25.	C
11.	A	26.	D
12.	D	27.	C
13.	D	28.	A
14.	D	29.	B
15.	C	30.	D

ELECTRICITY
EXAMINATION SECTION
TEST 1

DIRECTIONS: Each question or incomplete statement is followed by several suggested answers or completions. Select the one that BEST answers the question or completes the statement. *PRINT THE LETTER OF THE CORRECT ANSWER IN THE SPACE AT THE RIGHT.*

1. The one of the following items in which the metal alloy "Alnico" is *most likely* to be found is

    A. thermocouples
    B. heating elements
    C. wire-wound resistors
    D. permanent magnets

    1.____

2. Of the following devices, the one which, when inserted between a rectifier and its load, reduces the ripple current is the

    A. wave trap
    B. coupling transformer
    C. inverter
    D. filter

    2.____

3. The Q-factor (quality factor) of an inductor equals the

    A. product of its reactance and its resistance
    B. product of its inductance and its resistance
    C. ratio of its inductance to its resistance
    D. ratio of its reactance to its resistance

    3.____

4. Of the following types of screw heads, the one which requires a cross-slot screwdriver having 45-degree flukes and a sharp pointed head, is the

    A. Phillips
    B. Recessed
    C. Torque-set
    D. Reed and Prince

    4.____

5. Of the following, the *most likely* reason why loudspeakers in a public address system might produce a loud, howling noise when the input is a normal speaking voice, is

    A. feedback
    B. attenuation
    C. squelching
    D. transient current

    5.____

6. A megohmmeter of suitable voltage is used to test the condition of an A.C. electrolytic capacitor. Two readings are taken and the test leads are reversed between readings. The capacitor is discharged before and after the readings. The meter indications will stabilize at readings which are

    A. zero for one connection and high for the other, if the capacitor is defective
    B. high for one connection and zero for the other, if the capacitor is good
    C. zero for both connections, if the capacitor is good
    D. high for both connections, if the capacitor is good

    6.____

7. Of the following terms, the one which is most frequently used to describe circuits formed by etching metal foil deposited on a base of insulating material is the

   A. printed circuit
   B. wired circuit
   C. bread-board circuit
   D. prototype circuit

8. The PRIMARY function of a "zero sequence" current transformer, when installed in a four-wire A.G. power distribution system, is to detect

   A. ground faults
   B. metering errors
   C. phase sequences
   D. power factors

9. In three-phase rectifier systems, it is common practice to connect the power transformer with its primaries in _____ and its secondaries in _____.

   A. delta; delta
   B. delta; wye
   C. wye; delta
   D. wye; wye

10. The tap changer in a distribution transformer is normally used to change the

    A. voltage ratio
    B. insulating oil
    C. winding polarity
    D. impedance matching

11. The eddy currents in a distribution transformer can BEST be reduced by

    A. laminating the iron core
    B. polarizing both windings
    C. installing a secondary capacitor
    D. increasing the primary voltage

12. Of the following procedures, the one which is a precaution that should be taken when working with an instrument current transformer is:

    A. Short the primary before disconnecting it
    B. Short the secondary before disconnecting it
    C. Ground the primary after disconnecting it
    D. Ground the secondary after disconnecting it

13. If the line voltages across the load equal the phase voltages across the load in a balanced three-phase A.C. circuit, the load is connected in

    A. delta   B. Scott   C. star   D. wye

14. Of the following motors, the one MOST commonly used to correct a lagging power factor is the

    A. induction motor
    B. synchronous motor
    C. series motor
    D. compound motor

15. The one of the following motors which *frequently* requires a D.C. supply for excitation is the

    A. capacitor motor
    B. shaded-pole motor
    C. wound-rotor motor
    D. synchronous motor

16. Of the following, the *most likely* reason why a compound D.C. motor is running more slowly at full load than it normally does is that its

    A. line voltage is too high
    B. series field bucks the shunt field
    C. shunt field is open
    D. armature has a short

17. Suppose a newly installed D.C. shunt motor rotates in the wrong direction. This condition can be corrected by reversing the connections to

    A. the armature and the field only
    B. either the armature or the field
    C. the armature, the field, and the line
    D. the line only

18. Switches used to disconnect generator or synchronous motor fields are frequently designed to connect which of the following? A discharge

    A. *resistor* across the commutator before opening the circuit
    B. *capacitor* across the commutator after opening the circuit
    C. *capacitor* across the field after opening the circuit
    D. *resistor* across the field before opening the circuit

19. After grinding a new surface on a commutator having mica-insulated copper bars, it is good practice to

    A. side-cut the bars and under-cut the mica
    B. feather-edge the bars and create mica fins
    C. under-cut the bars and side-cut the mica
    D. dress both the bars and the mica until they are flush with each other

20. In a lap-wound D.C. motor armature, the two ends of each armature coil are *usually* connected to commutator segments that are

    A. adjacent to each other
    B. opposite from each other
    C. separated by 90 electrical degrees
    D. separated by 360 electrical degrees

KEY (CORRECT ANSWERS)

1. B
2. D
3. D
4. D
5. A

6. D
7. A
8. A
9. B
10. A

11. A
12. B
13. A
14. B
15. D

16. D
17. B
18. D
19. A
20. A

TEST 2

DIRECTIONS: Each question or incomplete statement is followed by several suggested answers or completions. Select the one that BEST answers the question or completes the statement. *PRINT THE LETTER OF THE CORRECT ANSWER IN THE SPACE AT THE RIGHT.*

1. The direction of rotation of an A.C. repulsion motor can be reversed by 1.____
   A. reversing the line connections
   B. reversing the field connections
   C. shifting the shading coil past the main stator winding
   D. shifting the brushes to the reverse side of the neutral

2. The number of threads per inch usually found on the threaded section of a 1-inch micrometer caliper's spindle, is 2.____
   A. 25   B. 40   C. 75   D. 100

3. Three-phase A.G. motors with six leads, when connected to star-delta starters, are usually run _____ and started _____. 3.____
   A. delta; star
   B. delta; delta
   C. star; delta
   D. star; star

4. In a typical three-phase A.C. electrically-operated magnetic motor starter, the auxiliary contact, the start button, and the stop button are usually connected so that the auxiliary contact is in 4.____
   A. *series* with both buttons
   B. *series* with the start button
   C. *parallel* with both buttons
   D. *parallel* with the start button

5. Of the following classifications of insulating materials used in electrical machinery, the one with the HIGHEST maximum safe-operating temperature is class 5.____
   A. A   B. B   C. H   D. O

6. Of the following features, the one which makes it possible to operate certain circuit breakers remotely, regardless of load, is the 6.____
   A. shunt trip
   B. gutter tap
   C. limiter lug
   D. thermal element

7. Thermal magnetic circuit breakers usually provide _____ overload protection and _____ short circuit protection. 7.____
   A. instantaneous; instantaneous
   B. inverse time delay; instantaneous
   C. inverse time delay; inverse time delay
   D. instantaneous; inverse time delay

8. Following are sets of branch circuit numbers for an 18-circuit, sequence-phased, lighting panelboard equipped with single-phase circuit breakers in each circuit and connected to a three-phase, four-wire feeder.
The set which consists of circuit numbers which are usually all connected to the same phase is

   A. 1, 2, 3, 4, 5, 6
   B. 1, 3, 5, 7, 9, 11
   C. 2, 4, 6, 8, 10, 12
   D. 1, 2, 7, 8, 13, 14

9. Unless otherwise specified, lighting panelboard boxes are usually manufactured with knockouts *only* on the

   A. top, bottom, and back
   B. top, and both sides
   C. bottom, and both sides
   D. top and bottom

10. When using a 12-point box wrench to turn a nut, the MINIMUM angle through which the wrench must be swung before the next set of points can be fitted to the corners of the nut, is

    A. 15°
    B. 30°
    C. 45°
    D. 60°

11. Suppose that the floor plans for a certain building are drawn to a scale of 1/8" = 1'0". On these plans the distance between two symbols representing receptacle outlets measures 2 7/8" on an ordinary ruler.
The actual distance between the two receptacle outlets installed at these locations should be

    A. 2 7/8 inches
    B. 2 feet 7 inches
    C. 16 feet
    D. 23 feet

12. Of the following combinations of switches, the one usually used when it is necessary to control a lighting fixture from five different locations, is

    A. two three-way switches and three four-way switches
    B. two four-way switches and three three-way switches
    C. five three-way switches
    D. five four-way switches

13. Of the following, the MOST common use for a Wheatstone bridge is to

    A. shunt leakage currents
    B. measure resistances
    C. bypass faulty components
    D. support scaffolds

14. Suppose that, when both test-tips of a neon-glow lamp tester are properly placed across a live circuit, only one of its electrodes glows. Of the following, the *most likely* reason for this is that the circuit is

    A. D.C., and the glowing electrode is connected to the negative side
    B. D.C., and the glowing electrode is connected to the positive side
    C. A.C., and the voltage is too low to permit both electrodes to glow
    D. A.C., and the glowing electrode is connected to the grounded neutral

15. The specific gravity of a fully charged lead acid storage battery is, *most nearly,*

    A. 1.000
    B. 1.150
    C. 1.280
    D. 1,830

16. The three regions in a junction transistor cross-section are *commonly* known as the

    A. cathode, grid, and emitter regions
    B. collector, emitter, and base regions
    C. base, grid, and plate regions
    D. emitter, cathode, and screen regions

17. An axially color-coded fixed resistor, having neither a gold nor a silver marking, is only accurate to within _____ percent of its marked value.

    A. 5   B. 10   C. 15   D. 20

18. Of the following sizes of machine screws, the one indicating the GREATEST number of threads per inch, is the

    A. No. 6 - 32
    B. No. 10 - 24
    C. No. 14 - 18
    D. No. 30 - 14

19. The number of threads per inch MOST commonly used on 3/4 inch rigid conduit is

    A. 27   B. 18   C. 14   D. 8

20. Of the following three-phase, 4-wire, secondary voltage combinations, the one MOST frequently used in industrial plants and commercial buildings, is _____ volts.

    A. 138/240   B. 208/260   C. 277/480   D. 347/600

KEY (CORRECT ANSWERS)

1. D	11. D
2. B	12. A
3. A	13. B
4. D	14. A
5. C	15. C
6. A	16. B
7. B	17. D
8. D	18. A
9. D	19. C
10. B	20. C

TEST 3

DIRECTIONS: Each question or incomplete statement is followed by several suggested answers or completions. Select the one that BEST answers the question or completes the statement. PRINT THE LETTER OF THE CORRECT ANSWER IN THE SPACE AT THE RIGHT.

1. The total resistance of ten 5-ohm resistors connected in parallel is 1.____
   A. 50 ohms   B. 10 ohms   C. 2 ohms   D. 0.5 ohm

2. The power consumed by a 100-ohm resistor carrying a D.C. current of 5 amperes is 2.____
   A. 4 watts   B. 20 watts   C. 500 watts   D. 2500 watts

3. The impedance of a series circuit consisting of a 6-ohm resistor, a 12-ohm capacitive reactance, and a 4-ohm inductive reactance, is 3.____
   A. 22 ohms   B. 18 ohms   C. 16 ohms   D. 10 ohms

4. The capacitive reactance of a 60-Hertz A.C. circuit consisting of a 50 microfarad capacitor is, *most nearly*, 4.____
   A. .0188 ohm   B. .0200 ohm   C. 53 ohms   D. 3,000 ohms

5. A coil having an inductive reactance of 100 ohms is designed to operate satisfactorily at 120 volts and 60 Hertz. This coil has negligible resistance and is energized from a 120-volt, 25-Hertz source. In order not to exceed rated current, it will be necessary to add a resistance in series with the coil. The *value* of this resistance is, *most nearly*, 5.____
   A. 40 ohms   B. 60 ohms   C. 80 ohms   D. 100 ohms

6. The power factor of a single-phase A.G. circuit consuming 1,800 watts at 120 volts while drawing 20 amperes, is 6.____
   A. .50   B. .75   C. .86   D. 1.33

7. The MAXIMUM instantaneous voltage that occurs across a circuit which is connected to a common 120-volt, 60-Hertz, single-phase supply, is, *most nearly*, 7.____
   A. 120 volts   B. 141 volts   C. 170 volts   D. 208 volts

8. The line current in a three-phase, four-wire 120/208 volt feeder circuit, supplying a balanced 120-volt lighting load totaling 36 kilowatts, *is, most nearly*, 8.____
   A. 300 amps   B. 173 amps   C. 100 amps   D. 57 amps

9. Three equal resistors connected in delta across a three-phase, 120/208 volt supply, drawing line currents of 30 amperes, will each have a resistance of, *most nearly*, 9.____
   A. 4 ohms   B. 12 ohms   C. 33 ohms   D. 70 ohms

10. The full load-line current of a squirrel cage induction motor rated at 2 H.P., having an efficiency of 70%, a power factor of 70%, and connected to a 3-phase, 208-volt, 60-Hertz supply, is *most nearly*

    A. 1.5 amperes   B. 5.0 amperes
    C. 8.5 amperes   D. 14.5 amperes

11. A D.C. circuit consists of an unknown resistance in series with a five-ohm resistor. It is found that when a voltmeter is placed across the five-ohm resistor, it reads 40 volts.
If the voltmeter reads 54 volts when placed across the unknown resistance, the value of the unknown resistance is, *most nearly*,

    A. 3.7 ohms   B. 6.8 ohms   C. 7.0 ohms   D. 14.0 ohms

12. If the diameter of a copper wire is twice the diameter of another copper wire of the same length, the resistance of the first wire will be _____ the resistance of the second wire.

    A. 1/4 of   B. 1/2 of
    C. 2 times   D. 4 times

13. A defective 120-volt, 1-kilowatt electric heater needs a new heating element. If this element is to consist of a continuous length of nichrome wire having a resistance of 1.5 ohms per foot, the length of this wire should be, *most nearly*,

    A. 3.5 feet   B. 8.5 feet   C. 9.5 feet   D. 14.5 feet

14. The diameter of a round copper bus-bar having a circular cross-section with an area of 250,000 circular mils, is, *most nearly*,

    A. 1/4 inch   B. 1/2 inch   C. 2 1/2 inches   D. 5 inches

15. The number of circular mils in a copper wire whose diameter is 1/8" is, *most nearly*,

    A. 125,000   B. 15,625   C. 3,140   D. 387

16. A 2"-wide rectangular copper bus-bar is to carry 500 amperes D.C. without exceeding a maximum allowable current density of 1,000 amperes. The MINIMUM thickness of this bus-bar must be

    A. 1/8 inch   B. 3/16 inch   C. 1/4 inch   D. 1/2 inch

17. A three-phase, 60-Hertz A.C. squirrel cage induction motor will have a synchronous speed of 1200 rpm if it has

    A. 4 poles   B. 6 poles   C. 8 poles   D. 10 poles

18. The speed of a four-pole, three-phase, 60-Hertz, squirrel cage induction motor running with a slip of 5.6% will be, *most nearly*,

    A. 850 rpm   B. 1700 rpm   C. 2550 rpm   D. 3400 rpm

19. The full load-line current of a 1-horsepower, single-phase, 60-Hertz, A.C. motor, having an efficiency of 70 percent, is, *most nearly*, _____ amperes

    A. 4   B. 6   C. 8   D. 10

20. The percent regulation of a single-phase transformer whose secondary terminal voltage varies from 126 volts at no load, to 120 volts at full load, is, *most nearly*, _____ percent.
    A. 3.6 B. 4.8 C. 5.0 D. 6.0

KEY (CORRECT ANSWERS)

1. D	11. B
2. D	12. A
3. D	13. C
4. C	14. B
5. B	15. B
6. B	16. C
7. C	17. B
8. C	18. B
9. B	19. C
10. C	20. C

TEST 4

DIRECTIONS: Each question or incomplete statement is followed by several suggested answers or completions. Select the one that BEST answers the question or completes the statement. PRINT THE LETTER OF THE CORRECT ANSWER IN THE SPACE AT THE RIGHT.

1. When preparing fresh electrolyte for a lead-acid storage battery, it is considered best to pour the concentrated acid into the water rather than adding water to the concentrated acid. The MAIN reason for following this sequence is to prevent 1.____
    A. corrosion
    B. sedimentation
    C. loss of concentrated acid
    D. production of excessive heat

2. Fire extinguishers suitable for use on an electrical fire should be identified by a 2.____
    A. five-pointed star containing the letter "D"
    B. triangle containing the letter "A"
    C. square containing the letter "B"
    D. circle containing the letter "C"

3. The SMALLEST size of rigid conduit that may be installed when wiring for new branch circuit receptacle outlets is 3.____
    A. 1 inch B. 3/4 inch C. 1/2 inch D. 3/8 inch

4. Of the following, the *color* of a fixed equipment ground wire should be 4.____
    A. white B. black C. red D. green

5. Of the following, the HEAVIEST fixture that may be supported directly from its outlet box is one weighing 5.____
    A. 25 pounds B. 35 pounds C. 45 pounds D. 55 pounds

6. The SMALLEST size of copper wire that may be used as a system ground on an A.C. service is 6.____
    A. No. 6 B. No. 8 C. No. 10 D. No. 12

7. The SMALLEST size of feeder conductor that must be stranded if installed in raceways is 7.____
    A. No. 6 B. No. 2 C. No. 1/0 D. 250 MCM

8. Of the following locations, the *ones* usually classified as Class I hazardous locations are 8.____
    A. rooms used for spray painting
    B. woodworking plants
    C. cotton-waste storage rooms
    D. janitor's sink closets

9. In relation to the allowable current carrying capacity of wiring it is protecting, the MAXIMUM value that an instantaneous magnetic trip circuit breaker may be set for is _____ of the allowable current-carrying capacity. 9.____
    A. 75% B. 100% C. 125% D. 150%

10. When installed in vertical raceways, 500 MCM feeders must be supported at intervals NOT greater than

   A. 100 feet   B. 75 feet   C. 50 feet   D. 25 feet

11. Sections of existing conduit exceeding 3 feet in length are being used to rewire for increased load, using more than four non-lead covered conductors. The MAXIMUM percentage of the conduit's cross-sectional area which may be occupied by these conductors is

   A. 60%   B. 50%   C. 40%   D. 30%

12. The MAXIMUM length of armored cable that may be exposed at the terminal connections of a ventilating fan located in a fan room is

   A. 8 feet   B. 6 feet   C. 4 feet   D. 2 feet

13. The MAXIMUM allowable current rating for a 250-volt ferrule contact, cartridge fuse is _____ amperes.

   A. 200   B. 100   C. 60   D. 30

14. An approved attachment plug and receptacle may be used as the controller for a portable motor whose horsepower rating is NOT larger than

   A. 1/4 HP   B. ⅓ HP   C. 1/2 HP   D. 1 HP

15. A printed or typed directory must be mounted in an approved manner on the door of a panelboard having more than _____ circuits.

   A. 4   B. 6   C. 8   D. 10

16. Surface metal raceways should NOT be used for wires larger than

   A. No. 6   B. No. 8   C. No. 10   D. No. 12

17. The MINIMUM length of a pull box with knockouts, installed in a run of 1 1/2-inch conduit containing a set of No 4 RH lighting panel feeders, is

   A. 24 inches   B. 18 inches   C. 12 inches   D. 6 inches

18. Suppose you find some of the conductors in a cutout box identified by means of a half-inch wide band of yellow tape. Of the following, it is *most likely* that these identified conductors are in circuits that are

   A. direct current   B. alternating current
   C. grounded   D. spares

19. The MINIMUM size of wire that may be used as fixture wire is

   A. No. 14   B. No. 16   C. No. 18   D. No. 20

20. The SMALLEST size of copper wire that may be used as an equipment ground if the branch circuit over-current device is rated at 20 amperes, is a

   A. No. 10   B. No. 12   C. No. 16   D. No. 18

KEY (CORRECT ANSWERS)

1. D
2. D
3. C
4. D
5. C

6. B
7. A
8. A
9. C
10. C

11. C
12. B
13. C
14. A
15. A

16. A
17. C
18. A
19. C
20. C

ELECTRICITY
EXAMINATION SECTION
TEST 1

DIRECTIONS: Each question or incomplete statement is followed by several suggested answers or completions. Select the one that BEST answers the question or completes the statement. *PRINT THE LETTER OF THE CORRECT ANSWER IN THE SPACE AT THE RIGHT.*

1. A prony brake is used to determine the

   A. output of a generator
   B. output of a transformer
   C. horsepower output of a motor
   D. input to a motor

   1._____

2. The direction of rotation of a shunt motor may be reversed by

   A. reversing the line wires
   B. reversing the shunt field leads
   C. reversing the residual magnetism
   D. placing the brushes on the neutral axis

   2._____

3. The torque of a series motor varies

   A. *directly* with the current on the line
   B. *inversely* with the current in the field
   C. *directly* with the current in the armature squared
   D. *inversely* with the armature current squared

   3._____

4. A no-field release is *generally* found in a

   A. three-point starting box
   B. four-point starting box
   C. magnetic switch
   D. thermal cut-out

   4._____

5. No voltage release is *generally* provided for

   A. in a three-point starter
   B. in a magnetic circuit breaker
   C. across the line starter
   D. in a four-point starter

   5._____

6. A D.C. 150-volt voltmeter whose resistance is 15,000 ohms may be used to read 300 volts by connecting a resistance in series whose value is

   A. 1,500 ohms   B. 30,000 ohms   C. 3,000 ohms   D. 15,000 ohms

   6._____

7. The horsepower of a D.C. motor is equal to

   A. $E \times I$ B. $E \times I \times EFF$ C. $\dfrac{E \times I}{746}$ D. $\dfrac{E \times I \times EFF}{746}$

   7._____

8. As the speed increases, the back e.m.f. of a shunt motor

   A. *decreases* the current taken by the motor
   B. *increases* until it equals the line voltage
   C. *does not change*
   D. *decreases*

   8._____

91

9. Split phase starting in single phase motor is used to

   A. divide the current equally between two circuits
   B. double the speed of the motor
   C. decrease the torque of the motor
   D. produce a rotating field

10. Capacitor motors are *usually* preferred to other single phase motors because of

    A. better speed regulation
    B. easy speed control
    C. higher starting power factor
    D. easier maintenance

11. A split phase induction motor is reversed by reversing the

    A. line wires
    B. starting winding
    C. starting and running windings
    D. rotor

12. The speed of a synchronous motor

    A. *increases* when the field current increases
    B. *decreases* when the field current increases
    C. *remains constant*
    D. *increases* when the field current decreases

13. The horsepower of a one horsepower single-phase motor whose efficiency is 90% is

    A. .9 H.P.   B. 1 H.P.   C. 1.1 B.P.   D. 1.8 H.P.

14. The output line voltage of three 208-volt, 1:1 transformers, connected wye-primary, delta-secondary, across a three-phase 208-volt line, is

    A. 208 volts   B. 240 volts   C. 60 volts   D. 120 volts

15. The output line voltage of three 208-volt, 1:1 transformers, connected delta-wye across a 208-volt line, is

    A. $120\sqrt{3}$ volts   B. 240 volts   C. 208 volts   D. $208\sqrt{3}$ volts

16. The output line voltage of three 120-volt, 1:2 transformers, connected delta-delta across a 120-volt line, is

    A. 120 volts   B. 240 volts   C. $120\sqrt{3}$ volts   D. $240\sqrt{3}$ volts

17. Potential transformers are used to

    A. *increase* the voltage output of a line
    B. *decrease* the voltage of the line to a safe value
    C. *decrease* the line voltage to a safe value for use with a voltmeter
    D. *regulate* the line voltage

18. Low power factor in an induction motor

    A. *increases* the current drawn by the motor
    B. *increases* the efficiency
    C. *reduces* the speed considerably
    D. *increases* the torque of the motor

19. The rotation of a three-phase induction motor is *reversed* by reversing

    A. all the line wires
    B. any two leads
    C. the motor
    D. the field connections

20. The *true* power of a three-phase load is

    A. 3 x E x I
    B. $\sqrt{3}$ x E x I x Efficiency
    C. $\frac{3E \times I \times EFF \times \text{Power Factory}}{746}$
    D. $\frac{\sqrt{3}E \times I \times EFF \times PF}{746}$

21. A 6-pole, 208-volt, synchronous motor connected to a 60-cycle line has a speed of

    A. 1800 R.P.M.   B. 3600 R.P.M.   C. 1200 R.P.M.   D. 900 R.P.M.

22. Series A.C. motors have a speed which

    A. is constant
    B. varies inversely with the load
    C. is controlled by a field rheostat
    D. is controlled by magnetic switches

23. Compensators are used to start motors at

    A. reduced voltage
    B. reduced speed
    C. reduced load
    D. maximum load

24. To obtain minimum speed, the field rheostat of a shunt motor MUST be set so that its resistance is

    A. minimum
    B. one-fourth of maximum
    C. one-half of maximum
    D. maximum

25. The power factor of single-phase induction motors may be *improved* by

    A. splitting the phase
    B. using shaded poles
    C. using condensers
    D. increasing the air gap between the rotor and the field windings

KEY (CORRECT ANSWERS)

1.	C	11.	B
2.	B	12.	C
3.	C	13.	B
4.	A	14.	D
5.	D	15.	D
6.	D	16.	B
7.	D	17.	C
8.	A	18.	A
9.	D	19.	B
10.	C	20.	D

21.	C
22.	B
23.	A
24.	A
25.	C

TEST 2

DIRECTIONS: Each question or incomplete statement is followed by several suggested answers or completions. Select the one that BEST answers the question or completes the statement. *PRINT THE LETTER OF THE CORRECT ANSWER IN THE SPACE AT THE RIGHT.*

1. The power output of a three-phase generator may be determined by 1.____
    A. a watt meter and a voltmeter
    B. two wattmeters
    C. a prony brake
    D. a three-phase watthourmeter

2. When load is added to a D.C. motor with interpoles, the brushes are 2.____
    A. shifted in the direction of rotation
    B. shifted in the direction opposite that of rotation
    C. placed at the neutral axis
    D. left in the same position

3. The current in the series field of a compound D.C. generator 3.____
    A. *increases* if the speed is increased
    B. *decreases* as load is added
    C. *decreases* as speed increases
    D. *increases* as load is added

4. A voltmeter may be used to measure 4.____
    A. low resistances
    B. the resistance of a motor armature
    C. the resistance of a series field
    D. the insulation resistance of a D.C. field

5. Ammeter shunts are used to 5.____
    A. increase the current through the ammeter coil
    B. supply a path of low resistance for the flow of current
    C. divide the current evenly between the instrument and the shunt
    D. reduce the error of the reading

6. Watthourmeters measure 6.____
    A. power
    B. volts x amperes
    C. energy
    D. time

7. If the constant of a wattmeter is 4, the *actual* power is 7.____
    A. $\frac{1}{4}$ the reading
    B. 4 times the reading
    C. $\sqrt{4}$ times the reading
    D. $\frac{1}{4} E \times I$

8. A cumulatively connected compound motor has the series field connected so that its magnetic field

   A. assists the shunt field
   B. opposes the shunt field
   C. compensates for the I.R. drop of the line
   D. reduces sparking

9. A three-phase, 4-wire, 208-volt distribution system supplies

   A. 120 volts
   B. 208 and 104 volts
   C. 208 and $\sqrt{3}$ x 208 volts
   D. 208 volts and $\sqrt{3}$ x 104 volts

10. The armature resistance of a 120-volt D.C.motor is .05 ohms. At normal speed it draws 20 amperes.
    The back e.m.f. at normal speed is

    A. 1 volt
    B. 20 volts
    C. 119 volts
    D. 6 volts

11. The reactance of a field coil whose inductance is 0.1 henry when connected to a 60-cycle source of power, is

    A. 377 ohms
    B. 3.77 ohms
    C. 37.7 ohms
    D. 3770 ohms

12. The speed regulation of a shunt motor *as compared to* that of a cumulative compound motor is

    A. poorer
    B. the same
    C. better
    D. much poorer

13. As the load of a squirrel cage motor is increased to full rated load, its power factor

    A. increases
    B. remains unchanged
    C. decreases a little
    D. decreases considerably

14. When load is added to a compound generator whose series field bucks the shunt field,

    A. its speed will increase
    B. the terminal voltage will rise
    C. voltage control will be impossible
    D. the terminal voltage will decrease

15. The number of pairs of poles in a 25-cycle generator revolving at 750 R.P.M. is

    A. 2
    B. 3
    C. 1
    D. 4

16. The grid in a triode radio tube controls the

    A. plate voltage
    B. flow of current in the plate circuit
    C. grid voltage
    D. filament voltage

17. A microampere is equivalent to

    A. 1,000,000 amperes
    B. .0000001 ampere
    C. .001 ampere
    D. 1,000 amperes

18. In radio, a continuous wave has   18._____

    A. equal amplitude for all cycles
    B. decreasing amplitude for each cycle
    C. a mixed amplitude
    D. a rising amplitude for each cycle

19. A microphone changes   19._____

    A. electrical current into sound
    B. the value of the current
    C. sound to electrical current
    D. the volume of the output

20. The photo-electric cell used for the sound system of motion picture machines *changes*   20._____

    A. sound into electrical energy
    B. light into sound
    C. light waves into electrical current
    D. sound waves into light

21. The resistance of a conductor   21._____

    A. depends upon the type of insulation
    B. is directly proportional to its length
    C. is changed with its method of installation
    D. is immaterial when asbestos insulation is used

22. The material offering the LEAST resistance to the flow of an electric current is   22._____

    A. gold   B. aluminum   C. silver   D. copper

23. The window of a 30 amp. plug fuse is   23._____

    A. hexagonal   B. octagonal   C. round   D. irregular

24. The MAXIMUM voltage permitted for type "R" wire is   24._____

    A. 300   B. 500   C. 600   D. 1000

25. The SMALLEST size wire permitted for fixture wiring is number   25._____

    A. 14   B. 16   C. 18   D. 20

KEY (CORRECT ANSWERS)

1.	B	11.	C
2.	D	12.	C
3.	D	13.	A
4.	D	14.	D
5.	B	15.	A
6.	C	16.	B
7.	B	17.	B
8.	A	18.	A
9.	A	19.	C
10.	C	20.	C

21. B
22. C
23. C
24. C
25. C

TEST 3

DIRECTIONS: Each question or incomplete statement is followed by several suggested answers or completions. Select the one that BEST answers the question or completes the statement. *PRINT THE LETTER OF THE CORRECT ANSWER IN THE SPACE AT THE RIGHT.*

1. In splicing solid duplex wire, the splice should be   1.____

    A. staggered   B. bunched   C. interwoven   D. tapered

2. Type SNA conductors are permitted in   2.____

    A. new installations only
    B. rewiring where space is not available in existing raceways
    C. old and new installations
    D. switchboard wiring only

3. A McIntire sleeve is *generally* used   3.____

    A. in hanging fixtures   B. to insulate splices
    C. as an aid in bending conduit   D. in splicing aerial wires

4. The code states that solderless conductors may   4.____

    A. not be used   B. be used
    C. be used with special permission only
    D. be used only for fixture splicing

5. The reason for using flux when soldering splices is to   5.____

    A. lower the melting point of the solder
    B. cause the joint to heat rapidly
    C. reduce the oxide on the wires
    D. prevent corrosion of the wires

6. If a person is rendered unconscious by an electric shock, one should break the electrical contact, call a physician, *and*   6.____

    A. make patient comfortable until physician arrives
    B. use prone-pressure method of resuscitation
    C. administer a stimulant
    D. rub patient's body to increase circulation

7. The hydrometer is used to measure   7.____

    A. specific gravity of liquids
    B. specific gravity of solids
    C. water pressure in motor-driven pumps
    D. the amount of water passing a given point in a given time

8. The voltage of a fully-charged lead storage cell is   8.____

    A. 1.5   B. 2.2   C. 1.25   D. 6

9. In a dry cell, manganese dioxide is used

   A. as an electrolyte
   B. to remove the hydrogen
   C. to generate hydrogen
   D. to prevent leakage through the zinc

10. Eddy currents can be reduced by

    A. using alternating current
    B. increasing the voltage
    C. using rubber mounts under solenoids
    D. laminating the magnetic circuit

11. A four-way switch can be substituted for a

    A. 3-circuit electrolier switch
    B. double pole snap switch
    C. 3-way switch
    D. 4-circuit electrolier switch

12. A synchroscope is used to

    A. parallel alternators
    B. measure efficiency
    C. view fast-moving objects
    D. check X-ray tubes

13. A Wheatstone bridge is in balance when the galvanometer needle reads

    A. zero   B. 100   C. 500   D. 1000

14. Insulation resistance is *generally* measured by a

    A. megger   B. magneto   C. trailer   D. bell and battery

15. The bleck system refers to

    A. connectors for neutral grids
    B. a railroad signal system
    C. a system of wiring radio networks
    D. transformer supply to isolated plants

16. In fluorescent lighting, the elements at each end of the tube are known as

    A. electrodes   B. chokes   C. ballasts   D. tubulations

17. In place of a starter on a fluorescent fixture, one can use a

    A. capacitor
    B. momentary contact switch
    C. condenser
    D. reactor

18. The method used in wiring the component luminous tubings in neon signs is

    A. series   B. parallel   C. series or parallel
    D. series parallel

19. Two small spheres of equal diameter have charges of 1.6×10^{-4} coulombs and 4.0×10^{-6} coulombs, respectively.
    If the centers of the spheres are spaced 0.4 meters apart, the electrical force existing between the two spheres in newtons is

    A. 3.6×10^1 B. 2.8×10^{-7} C. 3.0×10^{-8} D. 2.75×10^4

20. Switches controlling signs shall be placed   20.____

    A. at the service equipment
    B. within sight of the sign
    C. at the main entrance to the building
    D. in the office of the premises displaying the sign

21. A type "S" fuse is rated from   21.____

    A. 0-30 amps.   B. 30-60 amps.
    C. 60-100 amps.   D. over 500 volts

22. A 220-110 volt service feeds a lighting panel. Trouble has occurred which has caused the   22.____
    incandescent lights to burn dimly.
    The MOST probable cause is

    A. a blown fuse on one line leg   B. poor quality of the lamps
    C. 100% power factor   D. an open neutral factor

23. In charging Edison-type storage batteries, the two leads from the charger, marked plus   23.____
    and minus, respectively, are connected to the battery as follows:

    A. 1 minus lead to minus terminal, plus lead to plus terminal
    B. Minus lead to plus terminal, plus lead to minus terminal
    C. By interchanging the polarity
    D. As indicated on the nameplate on the charger, since chargers differ

24. The energy accumulated in a storage battery is   24.____

    A. electrical   B. chemical   C. kinetic   D. mechanical

25. Appliance branch circuit wires shall be no smaller than number   25.____

    A. 8   B. 10   C. 12   D. 14

KEY (CORRECT ANSWERS)

1.	A	11.	C
2.	D	12.	A
3.	D	13.	A
4.	B	14.	A
5.	C	15.	B
6.	B	16.	A
7.	A	17.	B
8.	B	18.	A
9.	B	19.	A
10.	D	20.	B

21. A
22. D
23. A
24. B
25. C

TEST 4

DIRECTIONS: Each question or incomplete statement is followed by several suggested answers or completions. Select the one that BEST answers the question or completes the statement. *PRINT THE LETTER OF THE CORRECT ANSWER IN THE SPACE AT THE RIGHT.*

1. Portable cords for stage lighting shall be of the type known as 1.____
   A. S B. SN C. R D. VC

2. The switch for the emergency lights of a theatre shall be located 2.____
   A. at the stage switchboard B. in the manager's office
   C. in the projection booth D. in the lobby

3. The purpose of bombarding a neon tube is to 3.____
   A. remove inpurities B. remove the tubulation
   C. test the tube D. provide space for the electrodes

4. To find the impedance in an inductive circuit, it is necessary to use the formula, 4.____
   A. $Z = 2\pi fl$
   B. $Z = \sqrt{R^2 \times W}$
   C. $Z = \sqrt{R^2 + (2\pi fl)^2}$
   D. $Z = \sqrt{3} \times E \times I \times PF$

5. An electro-magnet connected to a source of direct current will have 5.____
   A. resistance B. inductive reactance
   C. capacitative reactance D. impedance

6. The formula which will give an answer in watts is 6.____
   A. $\dfrac{HP \times 746}{E \times I \times EFF}$
   B. $\sqrt{3} \times E \times I \times PF$
   C. $2\pi FL$
   D. $\dfrac{E}{I} \times EFF$

7. A vibrating bell can be changed into a single stroke bell by 7.____
   A. connecting a conductor from contact point to the grounded binding post
   B. adjusting the contact point
   C. eliminating one of the coils
   D. rewinding the coils

8. A bell ringing transformer consists of 8.____
   A. two coils
   B. two coils and an iron core
   C. two coils of different-size wires and an iron core
   D. two coils and a metal case

9. Bells may be operated from a D.C. lighting line

   A. by a transformer
   B. by use of a lamp resistance
   C. under no circumstances
   D. by means of a rectifier

10. A strop key is MOST similar in operation to a

    A. double pole switch
    B. 3-way switch
    C. 4-way switch
    D. 2-circuit electrolier switch

11. An electro-reset annunciator has

    A. 2 coils per figure
    B. 1 coil per figure
    C. 1 coil and 1 permanent magnet per figure
    D. a manual reset arrangement

12. Locking relays may be used in

    A. open circuit burglar alarm systems only
    B. closed circuit burglar alarm systems only
    C. any type of burglar alarm system
    D. no burglar alarm system

13. The term, high potential, designates voltages of from

    A. 301 to 600 volts
    B. 601 to 2,000 volts
    C. 2,001 to 15,000 volts
    D. 601 to 5,000 volts

14. Under the National Electric Code, a 3-way switch is classified as a(n)

    A. single pole switch
    B. double pole switch
    C. 3-way switch
    D. electrolier switch

15. In an emergency, a 3-way switch may be replaced by a

    A. 2-circuit electrolier switch
    B. double pole switch
    C. 4-way switch
    D. 3-circuit electrolier switch

16. To replace a 4-way switch, we may use a

    A. double pole snap switch
    B. double pole double throw switch
    C. 3-circuit electrolier switch
    D. 4-way switch

17. A standard remote control switch may be operated by a

    A. single pole switch
    B. double pole switch
    C. 3-way switch
    D. momentary contact switch

18. A telephone book switch is similar in operation to a

    A. strop key
    B. locking type push button
    C. locking type relay
    D. 2-circuit electrolier switch

19. To replace a telephone transmitter, we may use a

    A. ribbon microphone
    B. carbon microphone
    C. condenser microphone
    D. velocity microphone

20. An induction coil is used in a telephone circuit to

    A. prevent high frequency current from returning to the battery
    B. increase the voltage
    C. prevent cross talk
    D. permit more than one conversation at a time

21. The MOST common type of private telephone system is

    A. common ringing - common talking
    B. selective ringing - common talking
    C. selective ringing - selective talking
    D. dial phone

22. Magnetoes as used in telephone systems

    A. supply current to the ringing circuit
    B. supply current to the talking circuit
    C. supplement the current supplied by the cells
    D. test the talking circuit

23. In connecting stranded wires under binding screws, BEST practice calls for

    A. twisting the ends and placing them under the binding screws
    B. placing the ends under the binding screws without twisting them
    C. twisting the ends, soldering them and placing them under the binding screw in the direction the screw tends to tighten
    D. soldering the strands and tightening under the binding screw in a counter-clockwise direction

24. A 600-volt cartridge fuse may be recognized by its

    A. blue label   B. green label
    C. red label   D. brown label

25. A plug fuse of less than 15 amperes may be recognized by its

    A. hexagonal window opening   B. round window opening
    C. square window opening   D. octagonal window opening

KEY (CORRECT ANSWERS)

1.	A	11.	A
2.	D	12.	C
3.	A	13.	D
4.	C	14.	A
5.	A	15.	C
6.	B	16.	B
7.	A	17.	D
8.	C	18.	A
9.	B	19.	B
10.	B	20.	B

21.	B
22.	A
23.	C
24.	C
25.	A

EXAMINATION SECTION
TEST 1

DIRECTIONS: Each question or incomplete statement is followed by several suggested answers or completions. Select the one that BEST answers the question or completes the statement. *PRINT THE LETTER OF THE CORRECT ANSWER IN THE SPACE AT THE RIGHT.*

1. A piece of No. 1/0 emery cloth should be used to sand the commutator of a D.C. dynamo   1._____
    A. when there is sparking at the brushes
    B. under no conditions
    C. when the commutator has a "chocolate" color
    D. only when the commutator has ridges

2. Compound D.C. generators connected in parallel are *generally* provided with   2._____
    A. 3 brushes   B. an equalizer
    C. no voltage relays   D. armature resistors

3. As compared with other types of A.C. motors, the advantage of the squirrel cage motor lies in its   3._____
    A. high starting torque   B. high power factor
    C. constant speed   D. simplicity

4. A counter E.M.F. starter is so named because   4._____
    A. the accelerating contactor has a high counter E.M.F.
    B. the accelerating relay depends upon the armature terminal voltage for operation
    C. it is used only on motors that build up a high C.E.M.F.
    D. it stops the motor by means of C.E.M.F.

5. There shall NOT be more than _____ quarter bends or their equivalent from outlet to outlet in rigid conduit.   5._____
    A. 3   B. 4   C. 5   D. 6

6. Armored cable may be imbedded in masonry in buildings under construction *provided*   6._____
    A. it is type AC   B. it is fastened securely
    C. it is type ACL   D. special permission is obtained

7. An armature core is laminated in order to reduce   7._____
    A. hysteresis loss   B. eddy current loss
    C. hysteresis and eddy current loss   D. impedance loss

8. The MOST efficient size of the "white" fluorescent lamps is   8._____
    A. 15 watts   B. 30 watts   C. 40 watts   D. 100 watts

9. Condensers are placed in parallel with fluorescent glow switches in order to   9._____
    A. reduce radio interference   B. reduce the arc
    C. compensate the power factor   D. increase the lamp life

10. The SMALLEST size wire that may be used on fire alarm systems is No. _____

    A. 18   B. 16   C. 14   D. 12

11. Under the National Electric Code, a 3-way switch is classified as a(n)

    A. single pole switch
    B. double pole switch
    C. 3-way switch
    D. electrolier switch

12. A capacitor start-and-run motor may be reversed by reversing the

    A. running and starting capacitor leads
    B. main winding leads
    C. line leads
    D. centrifugal switch leads

13. Opening a series field circuit while a compound motor is operating, will cause

    A. the motor to stop
    B. no noticeable change
    C. the motor to race
    D. the motor to slow down

14. Transformers for neon signs shall have a secondary voltage NOT exceeding

    A. 10,000 volts
    B. 15,000 volts
    C. 20,000 volts
    D. 25,000 volts

15. A capacitor of 10 ohms reactance and zero ohms resistance is connected in series with an inductance of 7 ohms reactance and 4 ohms resistance. The total impedance is

    A. 5 ohms   B. 7 ohms   C. 17 ohms   D. 21 ohms

16. The BEST way to start a large shunt motor is with a

    A. strong field
    B. weak field
    C. rheostat in series with the armature and the field
    D. starting compensator.

17. If an A.C. motor draws 50 amps., full load, the thermal cutout should be set at

    A. 75 amps.   B. 50 amps.   C. 62.5 amps.   D. 75 amps.

18. Using 1:1 ratio transformers at a given primary voltage, the HIGHEST secondary voltage may be obtained by connecting them

    A. Wye primary and Delta secondary
    B. Delta primary and Delta secondary
    C. Wye primary and Wye secondary
    D. Delta primary and Wye secondary

19. In an A.C. fire alarm system, the number of gongs allowed on a circuit is

    A. 10   B. 12   C. 14   D. 20

20. Appliance branch circuit wires shall be NO smaller than No.

    A. 8   B. 10   C. 12   D. 14

21. A current of 2 amperes in a resistor of 10 ohms will use electrical energy at the rate of _____ watts.

    A. 10   B. 20   C. 40   D. 80

22. 20-, 40-, and 50-ohm resistances are connected in series across a 110-volt D.C. supply; the current through the 20-ohm resistance is

    A. 5.5 amperes   B. 1 ampere   C. 2.2 ampers   D. 2.75 amperes

23. An electric circuit has four resistances of 20, 6, 30, and 12 ohms in parallel with each other. The combined resistance, in ohms, is

    A. 300   B. 30   C. 3   D. .3

24. The load for general illumination in apartment and multifamily dwellings is based on

    A. 1 1/2 watts per square foot of floor area
    B. 2 watts per square foot of floor area
    C. 3 watts per square foot of floor area
    D. 4 watts per square foot of floor area

25. Ventilation of battery rooms is necessary to

    A. keep the batteries cool
    B. prevent accumulation of explosive gases
    C. prevent deterioration of insulation
    D. supply oxygen to the room

KEYS (CORRECT ANSWERS)

1.	B	11.	A
2.	B	12.	B
3.	D	13.	A
4.	B	14.	B
5.	B	15.	A
6.	C	16.	A
7.	B	17.	C
8.	C	18.	D
9.	A	19.	A
10.	C	20.	C

21. B
22. B
23. C
24. B
25. B

TEST 2

DIRECTIONS: Each question or incomplete statement is followed by several suggested answers or completions. Select the one that BEST answers the question or completes the statement. *PRINT THE LETTER OF THE CORRECT ANSWER IN THE SPACE AT THE RIGHT.*

1. Dynamic braking is obtained in a motor by means of

   A. a magnetic brake
   B. a resistance connected across the armature after the current is disconnected
   C. reversing the armature
   D. reversing the field

2. The reason for using flux when soldering splices is to

   A. lower the melting point of the solder
   B. cause the joint to heat rapidly
   C. reduce the oxide on the wires
   D. prevent corrosion of the wires after soldering

3. A good ammeter should have

   A. very high resistance
   B. very low resistance
   C. low resistance
   D. high resistance

4. A good voltmeter should have

   A. very high resistance
   B. very low resistance
   C. low resistance
   D. high resistance

5. The MOST efficient type of polyphase motor to install for a large, slow speed, direct connected machine would be a

   A. wound rotor induction motor
   B. squirrel cage induction motor
   C. synchronous motor
   D. high torque induction motor

6. Mercury is added to the gas in a neon tube in order to produce the color

   A. gold   B. blue   C. white   D. red

7. An electromotive force will be built up in a conductor if it is moving

   A. in the same direction as magnetic lines of force
   B. in the opposite direction
   C. at right angles to the lines of force
   D. in any direction

8. The BEST choice of an A.C. motor to produce a high starting torque would be a

   A. synchronous motor
   B. split phase motor
   C. shaded pole motor
   D. wound rotor induction motor

9. The speed of a squirrel cage motor may be reduced by

   A. inserting a line resistance
   B. inserting a line reactance
   C. increasing the number of poles
   D. decreasing the number of poles

10. Three-point starting boxes provide for

    A. speed regulation   B. no field release
    C. no voltage release   D. phase reversal

11. If the #10 wire feeding a circuit were replaced with a #7 wire, the voltage drop would be reduced, *approximately,*

    A. 100%   B. 33%   C. 66%   D. 50%

12. Theatre footlight and border light branch circuits shall be so wired that in NO case will they carry *more than* _____ amperes.

    A. 10   B. 14   C. 20   D. 25

13. Which of the following is the outstanding feature of the Edison storage battery?

    A. A continued short circuit will not ruin the battery
    B. The lead plates are smaller
    C. It has a greater voltage output per cell
    D. It is less expensive than the automobile lead storage battery

14. An impedance coil is connected into a telephone circuit in the

    A. ringing circuit   B. talking circuit
    C. ringing and talking circuit
    D. secondary side of the induction coil

15. An electro reset annunciator has

    A. two coils per figure   B. one coil per figure
    C. one coil and one permanent magnet   D. manual reset arrangement

16. Locking relays may be used in

    A. open circuit burglar alarm systems only
    B. closed circuit burglar alarm systems only
    C. any type of burglar alarm system
    D. no burglar alarm system

17. The unit or electrical inductance is the

    A. henry   B. farad   C. joule   D. mho

18. The method used in calculating the total of resistances in series is NEAREST to that used in calculating

    A. condensers in series   B. inductances in parallel
    C. condensers in parallel   D. impedances in parallel

19. If 36,000 joules of work produce 5 amperes of current between two points for 60 seconds, what is the difference of potential between the two points, in volts?

    A. 600   B. 400   C. 120   D. 100

20. To measure a circuit current of 300 amps with a 100 amp ammeter, the shunt MUST have a MINIMUM capacity of _____ amps.

    A. 100   B. 200   C. 300   D. 400

21. A D.C. motor field coil connected first across a D.C. line and then across an A.C. line of equal voltage, will draw

    A. more current on D.C. than A.C.
    B. less current on D.C. than A.C.
    C. the same current on D.C. as on A.C.
    D. no current on A.C.

22. The single phase A.C. motor that produces the WEAKEST starting torque is the

    A. series A.C. motor   B. repulsion motor
    C. split phase motor   D. shaded pole motor

23. The D.C. generator whose terminal voltage falls off MOST rapidly when loaded is the _____ type.

    A. shunt   B. flat-compounded
    C. over-compounded   D. series

24. The E.M.F. produced by a primary cell depends on the

    A. size of the elements   B. amount of electrolyte
    C. distance between the elements
    D. materials used for the elements

25. A D.C. circuit consisting of 5 lamps in parallel draws 5 amperes; the current in *each* lamp is

    A. 1 ampere   B. 5 amperes
    C. determined by the resistance of the lamp
    D. 1/5 of an ampere

KEY (CORRECT ANSWERS)

1. B
2. C
3. B
4. A
5. C

6. B
7. C
8. D
9. C
10. B

11. D
12. B
13. A
14. B
15. A

16. C
17. A
18. C
19. C
20. B

21. A
22. D
23. A
24. D
25. C

TEST 3

DIRECTIONS: Each question or incomplete statement is followed by several suggested answers or completions. Select the one that BEST answers the question or completes the statement. *PRINT THE LETTER OF THE CORRECT ANSWER IN THE SPACE AT THE RIGHT.*

1. It is good practice to install a polarity reversing switch on a direct current fluorescent circuit to

   A. lessen ends blackening
   B. prevent one end from becoming dim
   C. ease starting
   D. prevent radio interference

   1._____

2. A 40-watt fluorescent lamp with necessary equipment may be satisfactorily operated from a direct current source of

   A. 110 volts
   B. 220 volts
   C. either voltage
   D. corrected power factor

   2._____

3. The National Electric Code provides that residential apartments be provided with receptacle outlets for *every* _____ feet of lineal wall space.

   A. 10   B. 15   C. 20   D. 25

   3._____

4. If a person is rendered unconscious by an electric shock, one should break the electrical contact, call a physician, *and*

   A. make patient comfortable until physician arrives
   B. use prone-pressure method of resuscitation
   C. administer a stimulant
   D. rub patient's body to increase circulation

   4._____

5. A 1 1/2" x 4" octagonal box may contain a MAXIMUM of

   A. 5 #14 conductors
   B. 7 #14 conductors
   C. 8 #14 conductors
   D. 11 #14 conductors

   5._____

6. A 1 1/2" x 4" square box may contain a MAXIMUM of

   A. 5 #14 conductors
   B. 7 #14 conductors
   C. 8 #14 conductors
   D. 11 #14 conductors

   6._____

7. Damaged cords for power tools should be

   A. coated with flux and covered with rubber tape
   B. repaired with insulating tape
   C. replaced
   D. shortened to remove the damaged section

   7._____

8. A source of direct current connected to a vibrating bell in series with the primary of an induction coil, will cause the secondary coil to produce

   A. alternating current
   B. direct current
   C. pulsating direct current
   D. interrupted direct current

9. Switches and attachment plugs installed in garages shall be AT LEAST _____ above the floor.

   A. 1 foot
   B. 2 feet
   C. 3 feet, 6 inches
   D. 4 feet

10. Rigid conduit used for electrical wiring is purchased in

    A. 10 feet lengths, including coupling
    B. 10 feet lengths
    C. 9'6" lengths
    D. no standard lengths

11. Switches controlling signs shall be placed

    A. at the service equipment
    B. in the office of the premises displaying the sign
    C. within sight of the sign
    D. at the main entrance to the building

12. A self-excited alternator has

    A. slip rings for the field excitation
    B. a storage battery for the field
    C. a winding connected to the commutator
    D. no coil for direct current

13. A copper wire twice the diameter of another has a carrying capacity of _____ as great.

    A. two times
    B. one-half
    C. four times
    D. eight times

14. The resistance of a copper bus bar is

    A. directly proportional to its length
    B. inversely proportional to its length
    C. negligible
    D. higher than that of gold

15. The resistance of a conductor depends upon the material it is made of *and*

    A. its temperature
    B. where it is used
    C. the ambient temperature
    D. method of installation

16. The positive terminal of an unmarked lead storage battery can *often* be identified by

    A. being larger than the negative
    B. being smaller than the negative
    C. removing the filling caps and looking at the plates
    D. using a "Y" box

17. The discharge voltage of an Edison storage cell is _____ volt(s).

    A. 1 B. 1.2 C. 2 D. 6

18. Voltmeters *often* have

    A. external shunts in parallel
    B. internal shunts
    C. internal resistance coils
    D. low resistance shunts

19. Selsyn motors are used

    A. to operate clocks from a direct current source
    B. at repeater stations
    C. as a generator for cathode ray tubes
    D. to charge storage batteries

20. The secondary of a current transformer

    A. is always opened with a connected load
    B. is never used with meters
    C. cannot be used on alternating current
    D. should never be opened while primary is energized

21. Circline is a development in

    A. fluorescent lighting
    B. raceways
    C. incandescent lighting
    D. insulating material

22. Neon signs operate on

    A. low voltage-high current
    B. high current-high voltage
    C. high voltage-low current
    D. low voltage-low current

23. Thermo electricity can be generated by heat applied to

    A. glass between two layers of aluminum foil
    B. two dissimilar metals
    C. two similar metals
    D. two lead plates in an electrolyte

24. To determine the power in a two-phase lighting and power system, the proper formula to use would be:

    A. $KW = \dfrac{E \times I \times PF}{1000}$
    B. $KW = 1.73 \times E \times I \times PF \times 1000$
    C. $KW = \dfrac{\sqrt{2} \times E \times I \times PF}{1000}$
    D. $KW = \dfrac{1.42 \times E \times W \times PF}{1000}$

25. An electric toaster operating on 120 volts has a resistance (hot) of 15 ohms. The wattage of the toaster is

    A. 1200 B. 1140 C. 1080 D. 960

KEY (CORRECT ANSWERS)

1. B
2. B
3. C
4. B
5. C

6. C
7. C
8. A
9. D
10. A

11. C
12. C
13. C
14. A
15. A

16. A
17. B
18. C
19. B
20. D

21. A
22. C
23. B
24. C
25. D

TEST 4

DIRECTIONS: Each question or incomplete statement is followed by several suggested answers or completions. Select the one that BEST answers the question or completes the statement. *PRINT THE LETTER OF THE CORRECT ANSWER IN THE SPACE AT THE RIGHT.*

1. When using lead cable, the inner radius of the bend shall be *no less than* _____ times the internal diameter of the conduit.

    A. four B. six C. eight D. ten

2. A telephone hook switch is similar in operation to a

    A. strop key
    B. locking type push button
    C. locking type relay
    D. two circuit electrolier switch

3. The "dielectric" of a condenser is the

    A. air surrounding the condenser
    B. material separating the plates
    C. voltage impressed on the condenser
    D. lines of force established by the current

4. The depolarizing substance in the dry cell is

    A. manganese dioxide
    B. ammonium chloride
    C. zinc chloride
    D. lead oxide

5. The SMALLEST wattage fluorescent lamp manufactured for home use is

    A. 6 B. 8 C. 9 D. 15

6. The Carter system of connecting three-way switches for lighting

    A. will not operate lamps in parallel
    B. is not permitted under the National Electric Code
    C. will not operate when used in conjunction with a pilot light
    D. will not operate lamps in series

7. The material offering the LEAST resistance to the flow of an electric current is

    A. iron B. aluminum C. German silver D. zinc

8. To replace a four-way switch, we may use the following type:

    A. Double pole snap
    B. Double pole, double throw
    C. Three-circuit electrolier
    D. Three-way switch

9. The LARGEST size conductor permitted in surface metal raceways is No.

    A. 10 B. 8 C. 6 D. 4

10. The energy accumulated in a storage battery is

    A. electrical B. chemical C. kinetic D. mechanical

2 (#4)

11. A strop key is MOST similar in operation to the following switch:

    A. Double pole
    B. Three-way
    C. Four-way
    D. Two circuit electrolier

12. Compensators are used to start motors at

    A. reduced voltage
    B. reduced speed
    C. reduced load
    D. increased voltage

13. A self-excited D.C. shunt generator is operating properly in clockwise rotation. If the direction of rotation is reversed, the

    A. brush polarity will reverse
    B. field polarity will reverse
    C. generator will fail to build up voltage
    D. output voltage will be the same in magnitude

14. If the intake port on an oil burner blower were closed, the motor would

    A. slow down
    B. require more current
    C. heat up
    D. require less current

15. In the event of a burnout of one single-phase transformer on a 3-phase, Wye-connected system, you can

    A. connect the remaining two in "delta"
    B. connect the remaining two "Scott"
    C. connect the remaining two "Open Wye"
    D. not connect them to obtain 3-phase with same voltage

16. The short circuited coil imbedded in the pole face of an A.C. contactor is used to

    A. blow out the arc
    B. reduce residual magnetism
    C. close the contactor
    D. reduce noise and vibration

17. A motor that is built for plugging service

    A. has a built-in brake
    B. helps to compensate power factor
    C. may be connected in reverse from full speed forward
    D. has built-in reduction gears

18. Eleven #14 conductors are permitted in a 1" conduit

    A. in apartment house risers
    B. under all conditions
    C. at no time
    D. for conductors between a motor and its controller

19. The number of mogul sockets on a two-wire branch circuit shall NOT exceed

    A. 8   B. 7   C. 6   D. 5

20. A 1 1/2" x 3 1/4" octagonal box may contain a MAXIMUM of

    A. 5 #14 conductors
    B. 7 #14 conductors
    C. 8 #14 conductors
    D. 11 #14 conductors

21. The average value of an alternating current is equal to its MAXIMUM value *times*   21.____

   A. 1.7232   B. .707   C. .636   D. 1.41

22. In a D.C. fire alarm system, the number of gongs allowed on a circuit is   22.____

   A. 10   B. 12   C. 13   D. 20

23. If the total resistance of the wire wound on a bipolar armature is 2 ohms, the armature resistance is _____ ohm(s).   23.____

   A. 1   B. 2   C. 1/2   D. 4

24. Increasing the field excitation of a synchronous motor will cause the   24.____

   A. motor to speed up
   B. motor to slow down
   C. current to lead
   D. voltage to lead

25. Mercury rectifiers have   25.____

   A. mercury anodes
   B. the positive terminal at the cathode
   C. high tank pressure
   D. one anode always

KEY (CORRECT ANSWERS)

1. D		11. B	
2. A		12. A	
3. B		13. C	
4. A		14. C	
5. A		15. C	
6. B		16. B	
7. B		17. C	
8. B		18. D	
9. C		19. B	
10. B		20. C	

21. C
22. C
23. C
24. B
25. C

TELECOMMUNICATIONS TERMS

bit rate *or* **baud rate** *n*. The speed (measured in *bits per second* [**BPS**], *kilobits per second* [**KBPS**], etc.) at which information can be transmitted over a given medium or by given equipment.

broad·cast·ing sat·el·lite ser·vi·ces [**BSS**] *n*. A radio-communications service in which signals transmitted or retransmitted by *satellites* are intended for direct reception by the general public. Also *satellite direct broadcasting*.

bund·led rates *n*. Rates in which the various rate elements that comprise the service are consolidated, making them indistinguishable.

cel·lu·lar mo·bile ra·di·o *n*. A form of portable telephone service that allows mobile radio telephones to both initiate and receive calls with private line quality. A metropolitan area is divided into "cells", each served by a low power radio transmitter that is linked to other transmitters by computer.

cen·tral of·fice [**CO**] **line** *n*. A circuit linking a customer with the local operating company's central office switching equipment; often *local loop*, or simply *line*, *phone line*, or *outside line*.

cir·cuit *n*. A two-way communications path.

co·ax·i·al ca·ble *n*. A cable composed of an inner wire conductor surrounded by a hollow cylindrical conductor with layers of insulation between them. Coaxial cable has high *baud rate* capacity and is usually required for applications such as cable television.

com·mon car·ri·er *n*. In telecommunications, a supplier that provides telecommunications services to the public, subject to state and Federal Communications Commission regulations. A *specialized common carrier* [**SCC**] provides intercity private line service in competition with established carriers. Any carrier other than American Telephone & Telegraph Co. is referred to as an *other common carrier* [**OCC**]; one that resells service bought wholesale from another carrier, rather than building and operating its own transmission facilities, is a *resale common carrier* [**RCC**].

com·mu·ni·ty an·ten·na tel·e·vi·sion [**CATV**] *n*. The original cable television service, which consisted primarily of capturing over-the-air broadcast signals and feeding them to linked customers in areas of poor reception.

in·te·grat·ed cir·cuit *n*. A single piece of silicon on which any number of transistors are directly etched along with the connections between them. This allows for whole sections of a computer, such as logic or memory components, to be contained within one chip. In *very large scale integration* [**VLSI**], the contents of hundreds of *integrated circuits* are etched on a single chip.

in·ter·ex·change serv·ice *n*. Telephone service between a point or points located in one *exchange area* and a point or points located in another or multiple exchange areas. Under the AT&T 1982 Consent Decree, service provided between a *local access and transport area* (LATA) and a point outside that LATA.

in·ter·na·tion·al re·cord car·ri·er [**IRC**] *n*. Formerly, a carrier that provided only international telecommunications services other than voice communications (e.g. data, Telex, facsimile transmission). The FCC recently lifted restrictions limiting IRCs to provision of record services and allowed them to offer voice communications as well. This decision (the Overseas Communications Services decision) also removed the limitation on AT&T to provide only voice transmission, enabling them to offer record and data services as well.

lo·cal ac·cess and trans·port ar·e·a [**LATA**] *n*. Geographic regions that subdivide the post-divestiture service areas of the 22 Bell operating companies. All telephone service within a LATA is *exchange service*, while service between LATAs is *interexchange service*. Bell operating companies are forbidden by the divestiture agreement to offer service between LATAs.

lo·cal loop *n*. A circuit connecting equipment to a switching facility or distribution point; for telephones, a *central office line*.

meas·ured lo·cal serv·ice *n*. A method of pricing local telephone service based on the number, the duration, the time of day, and the distance of calls within the local exchange area instead of a flat, all-inclusive rate.

mes·sage switch·ing *n*. The technique of receiving a message at a switching point, storing it until the proper outgoing line is available, and then transmitting it to the intended recipient.

mes·sage toll serv·ice [**MTS**] *n*. A nonprivate line intrastate and interstate long distance telephone service that permits local subscribers to establish two-way service on a message-by-message basis.

mi·cro·com·put·er *n*. Usually an eight- or 16-bit machine which can be used on a stand—alone basis or as an intelligent terminal, containing at least one microprocessor plus other supporting circuitry; much smaller than a *minicomputer*. PCs are an example of a microcomputer.

mi·cro·proc·es·sor *n*. An integrated circuit chip which contains the electronics of a *central processor unit*; the "brain" of a microcomputer.

mi·cro·wave *n*. Short electromagnetic waves at frequencies of 1,000 megahertz or greater, the highest portion of the radio range nearest to infrared light. Such signals can be transmitted between two points only if there is a *line of sight*, i.e. no intervening solid object.

min·i·com·put·er *n*. A computer smaller than a *mainframe*, often dedicated to one type of task. A typical *PBX* is a specialized type of minicomputer.

pack·et switch·ing *n*. A data communications switching and transmission system whereby an input data stream is broken into uniformly sized "packets" to which are appended addressing information, sequence counts, and error controls. Packets are transmitted independently through the network; at the receiving end the individual packets are resequenced and recombined into the output data stream. The effect is like sending a football team across town in a fleet of Toyotas instead of one enormous bus: The smaller cars are more maneuverable, easier to park, are less inclined to tie up traffic, and can go by different routes if necessary, permitting greater overall efficiency. The advantages of packet switching are analogous.

pri·vate (au·to·mat·ic) branch ex·change [**PBX** *or* **PABX**] *n*. A computerized device that switches a customer's "inside" communications traffic and links a private network to the public telephone network and various *carriers*. Some PBXs add to their basic task features such as direct-access inward dialing, automatic least-cost routing of toll calls, speed dialing, conference calling, call forwarding, and others.

ra·di·o fre·quen·cy [**RF**] **spec·trum** *n*. The portion of the electromagnetic spectrum lowest in frequency (below visible light) in which electromagnetic impulses can be radiated through space. Nearly all kinds of radio, television, radar, and other communications media such as *microwaves* use frequencies in this spectrum. The lower the *frequency*, the longer the *wavelength*, and the greater the signal's ability to pass through solid objects, but the slower the achievable *baud rates*.

sat·el·lite *n*. Any object which circles the Earth; usually, a device placed in orbit for some purpose, including telecommunications, broadcasting, weather observation, geodetic surveying, navigation, reconnaissance, sensing and others. Communications satellites usually must be in *geosynchronous orbit* to be useful—that is, they must circle the earth at the same ground speed as the earth's rotation, effectively remaining "fixed" over one point on the surface at the equator. Geosynchronous orbits are very high, and expensive and difficult to achieve and there are physical limits to the total number of satellites that may occupy them. Ground stations that send signals to satellites are *uplinks*; those that receive signals from satellites are *downlinks*.

sep·a·ra·tions *n*. The process by which telephone industry costs are allocated between interstate operations, subject to FCC jurisdiction, and intrastate operations, subject to state regulatory authority.

shared us·er *n*. One of several users in a nonprofit arrangement that collectively subscribe to a private line service of a carrier and share the costs and use of the service.

sig·nal *n*. Electromagnetic energy used to convey information.

tel·e·text *n*. A one-way information system in which textual and graphic material is generally conveyed as part of the television broadcast signal or over cable. [see *videotext*]

ter·mi·nal e·quip·ment *n*. Equipment capable of sending or receiving information over a telecommunications channel and converting that information for mechanical or human end use. The most common example: an ordinary telephone, called a *desk set* in the trade.

val·ue-add·ed car·ri·er *n*. a carrier that leases circuits from *common carriers* and then adds special services, features, or characteristics before retailing use of the circuits to a final user.

vid·e·o·disk *n*. A disk the size of a record album that stores large amounts of data, audio and video information in digital form.

vid·e·o·text *n*. A two-way computer-based information system in which a user is linked to a database by telephone line or cable. [see *teletext*]

ELECTRICAL TERMS AND FORMULAS

CONTENTS

	Page
TERMS	1
Agonic ...... Dielectric	1
Diode ...... Lead	2
Line of Force ...... Resistor	3
Retentivity ...... Wattmeter	4
FORMULAS	4
Ohm's Law for D-C Circuits	4
Resistors in Series	4
Resistors in Parallel	4
R-L Circuit Time Constant	5
R-C Circuit Time Constant	5
Comparison of Units in Electric and Magnetic Circuits	5
Capacitors in Series	5
Capacitors in Parallel	5
Capacitive Reactance	5
Impedance in an R-C Circuit (Series)	5
Inductors in Series	5
Inductors in Parallel	5
Inductive Reactance	5
Q of a Coil	5
Impedance of an R-L Circuit (Series)	5
Impedance with R, C, and L in Series	5
Parallel Circuit Impedance	5
Sine-Wave Voltage Relationships	5
Power in A-C Circuit	6
Transformers	6
Three-Phase Voltage and Current Relationships	6
GREEK ALPHABET	7
Alpha ...... Omega	7
COMMON ABBREVIATIONS AND LETTER SYMBOLS	8
Alternating Current (noun) ...... Watt	8

ELECTRICAL TERMS AND FORMULAS

Terms

AGONIC.—An imaginary line of the earth's surface passing through points where the magnetic declination is 0°; that is, points where the compass points to true north.

AMMETER.—An instrument for measuring the amount of electron flow in amperes.

AMPERE.—The basic unit of electrical current.

AMPERE-TURN.—The magnetizing force produced by a current of one ampere flowing through a coil of one turn.

AMPLIDYNE.—A rotary magnetic or dynamoelectric amplifier used in servomechanism and control applications.

AMPLIFICATION.—The process of increasing the strength (current, power, or voltage) of a signal.

AMPLIFIER.—A device used to increase the signal voltage, current, or power, generally composed of a vacuum tube and associated circuit called a stage. It may contain several stages in order to obtain a desired gain.

AMPLITUDE.—The maximum instantaneous value of an alternating voltage or current, measured in either the positive or negative direction.

ARC.—A flash caused by an electric current ionizing a gas or vapor.

ARMATURE.—The rotating part of an electric motor or generator. The moving part of a relay or vibrator.

ATTENUATOR.—A network of resistors used to reduce voltage, current, or power delivered to a load.

AUTOTRANSFORMER.—A transformer in which the primary and secondary are connected together in one winding.

BATTERY.—Two or more primary or secondary cells connected together electrically. The term does not apply to a single cell.

BREAKER POINTS.—Metal contacts that open and close a circuit at timed intervals.

BRIDGE CIRCUIT.—The electrical bridge circuit is a term referring to any one of a variety of electric circuit networks, one branch of which, the "bridge" proper, connects two points of equal potential and hence carries no current when the circuit is properly adjusted or balanced.

BRUSH.—The conducting material, usually a block of carbon, bearing against the commutator or sliprings through which the current flows in or out.

BUS BAR.—A primary power distribution point connected to the main power source.

CAPACITOR.—Two electrodes or sets of electrodes in the form of plates, separated from each other by an insulating material called the dielectric.

CHOKE COIL.—A coil of low ohmic resistance and high impedance to alternating current.

CIRCUIT.—The complete path of an electric current.

CIRCUIT BREAKER.—An electromagnetic or thermal device that opens a circuit when the current in the circuit exceeds a predetermined amount. Circuit breakers can be reset.

CIRCULAR MIL.—An area equal to that of a circle with a diameter of 0.001 inch. It is used for measuring the cross section of wires.

COAXIAL CABLE.—A transmission line consisting of two conductors concentric with and insulated from each other.

COMMUTATOR.—The copper segments on the armature of a motor or generator. It is cylindrical in shape and is used to pass power into or from the brushes. It is a switching device.

CONDUCTANCE.—The ability of a material to conduct or carry an electric current. It is the reciprocal of the resistance of the material, and is expressed in mhos.

CONDUCTIVITY.—The ease with which a substance transmits electricity.

CONDUCTOR.—Any material suitable for carrying electric current.

CORE.—A magnetic material that affords an easy path for magnetic flux lines in a coil.

COUNTER E.M.F.—Counter electromotive force; an e.m.f. induced in a coil or armature that opposes the applied voltage.

CURRENT LIMITER.—A protective device similar to a fuse, usually used in high amperage circuits.

CYCLE.—One complete positive and one complete negative alternation of a current or voltage.

DIELECTRIC.—An insulator; a term that refers to the insulating material between the plates of a capacitor.

ELECTRICAL TERMS AND FORMULAS

DIODE.—Vacuum tube—a two element tube that contains a cathode and plate; semiconductor—a material of either germanium or silicon that is manufactured to allow current to flow in only one direction. Diodes are used as rectifiers and detectors.

DIRECT CURRENT.—An electric current that flows in one direction only.

EDDY CURRENT.—Induced circulating currents in a conducting material that are caused by a varying magnetic field.

EFFICIENCY.—The ratio of output power to input power, generally expressed as a percentage.

ELECTROLYTE.—A solution of a substance which is capable of conducting electricity. An electrolyte may be in the form of either a liquid or a paste.

ELECTROMAGNET.—A magnet made by passing current through a coil of wire wound on a soft iron core.

ELECTROMOTIVE FORCE (e.m.f.).—The force that produces an electric current in a circuit.

ELECTRON.—A negatively charged particle of matter.

ENERGY.—The ability or capacity to do work.

FARAD.—The unit of capacitance.

FEEDBACK.—A transfer of energy from the output circuit of a device back to its input.

FIELD.—The space containing electric or magnetic lines of force.

FIELD WINDING.—The coil used to provide the magnetizing force in motors and generators.

FLUX FIELD.—All electric or magnetic lines of force in a given region.

FREE ELECTRONS.—Electrons which are loosely held and consequently tend to move at random among the atoms of the material.

FREQUENCY.—The number of complete cycles per second existing in any form of wave motion; such as the number of cycles per second of an alternating current.

FULL-WAVE RECTIFIER CIRCUIT.—A circuit which utilizes both the positive and the negative alternations of an alternating current to produce a direct current.

FUSE.—A protective device inserted in series with a circuit. It contains a metal that will melt or break when current is increased beyond a specific value for a definite period of time.

GAIN.—The ratio of the output power, voltage, or current to the input power, voltage, or current, respectively.

GALVANOMETER.—An instrument used to measure small d-c currents.

GENERATOR.—A machine that converts mechanical energy into electrical energy.

GROUND.—A metallic connection with the earth to establish ground potential. Also, a common return to a point of zero potential. The chassis of a receiver or a transmitter is sometimes the common return, and therefore the ground of the unit.

HENRY.—The basic unit of inductance.

HORSEPOWER.—The English unit of power, equal to work done at the rate of 550 foot-pounds per second. Equal to 746 watts of electrical power.

HYSTERESIS.—A lagging of the magnetic flux in a magnetic material behind the magnetizing force which is producing it.

IMPEDANCE.—The total opposition offered to the flow of an alternating current. It may consist of any combination of resistance, inductive reactance, and capacitive reactance.

INDUCTANCE.—The property of a circuit which tends to oppose a change in the existing current.

INDUCTION.—The act or process of producing voltage by the relative motion of a magnetic field across a conductor.

INDUCTIVE REACTANCE.—The opposition to the flow of alternating or pulsating current caused by the inductance of a circuit. It is measured in ohms.

INPHASE.—Applied to the condition that exists when two waves of the same frequency pass through their maximum and minimum values of like polarity at the same instant.

INVERSELY.—Inverted or reversed in position or relationship.

ISOGONIC LINE.—An imaginary line drawn through points on the earth's surface where the magnetic deviation is equal.

JOULE.—A unit of energy or work. A joule of energy is liberated by one ampere flowing for one second through a resistance of one ohm.

KILO.—A prefix meaning 1,000.

LAG.—The amount one wave is behind another in time; expressed in electrical degrees.

LAMINATED CORE.—A core built up from thin sheets of metal and used in transformers and relays.

LEAD.—The opposite of LAG. Also, a wire or connection.

ELECTRICAL TERMS AND FORMULAS

LINE OF FORCE.—A line in an electric or magnetic field that shows the direction of the force.

LOAD.—The power that is being delivered by any power producing device. The equipment that uses the power from the power producing device.

MAGNETIC AMPLIFIER.—A saturable reactor type device that is used in a circuit to amplify or control.

MAGNETIC CIRCUIT.—The complete path of magnetic lines of force.

MAGNETIC FIELD.—The space in which a magnetic force exists.

MAGNETIC FLUX.—The total number of lines of force issuing from a pole of a magnet.

MAGNETIZE.—To convert a material into a magnet by causing the molecules to rearrange.

MAGNETO.—A generator which produces alternating current and has a permanent magnet as its field.

MEGGER.—A test instrument used to measure insulation resistance and other high resistances. It is a portable hand operated d-c generator used as an ohmmeter.

MEGOHM.—A million ohms.

MICRO.—A prefix meaning one-millionth.

MILLI.—A prefix meaning one-thousandth.

MILLIAMMETER.—An ammeter that measures current in thousandths of an ampere.

MOTOR-GENERATOR.—A motor and a generator with a common shaft used to convert line voltages to other voltages or frequencies.

MUTUAL INDUCTANCE.—A circuit property existing when the relative position of two inductors causes the magnetic lines of force from one to link with the turns of the other.

NEGATIVE CHARGE.—The electrical charge carried by a body which has an excess of electrons.

NEUTRON.—A particle having the weight of a proton but carrying no electric charge. It is located in the nucleus of an atom.

NUCLEUS.—The central part of an atom that is mainly comprised of protons and neutrons. It is the part of the atom that has the most mass.

NULL.—Zero.

OHM.—The unit of electrical resistance.

OHMMETER.—An instrument for directly measuring resistance in ohms.

OVERLOAD.—A load greater than the rated load of an electrical device.

PERMALLOY.—An alloy of nickel and iron having an abnormally high magnetic permeability.

PERMEABILITY.—A measure of the ease with which magnetic lines of force can flow through a material as compared to air.

PHASE DIFFERENCE.—The time in electrical degrees by which one wave leads or lags another.

POLARITY.—The character of having magnetic poles, or electric charges.

POLE.—The section of a magnet where the flux lines are concentrated; also where they enter and leave the magnet. An electrode of a battery.

POLYPHASE.—A circuit that utilizes more than one phase of alternating current.

POSITIVE CHARGE.—The electrical charge carried by a body which has become deficient in electrons.

POTENTIAL.—The amount of charge held by a body as compared to another point or body. Usually measured in volts.

POTENTIOMETER.—A variable voltage divider; a resistor which has a variable contact arm so that any portion of the potential applied between its ends may be selected.

POWER.—The rate of doing work or the rate of expending energy. The unit of electrical power is the watt.

POWER FACTOR.—The ratio of the actual power of an alternating or pulsating current, as measured by a wattmeter, to the apparent power, as indicated by ammeter and voltmeter readings. The power factor of an inductor, capacitor, or insulator is an expression of their losses.

PRIME MOVER.—The source of mechanical power used to drive the rotor of a generator.

PROTON.—A positively charged particle in the nucleus of an atom.

RATIO.—The value obtained by dividing one number by another, indicating their relative proportions.

REACTANCE.—The opposition offered to the flow of an alternating current by the inductance, capacitance, or both, in any circuit.

RECTIFIERS.—Devices used to change alternating current to unidirectional current. These may be vacuum tubes, semiconductors such as germanium and silicon, and dry-disk rectifiers such as selenium and copper-oxide.

RELAY.—An electromechanical switching device that can be used as a remote control.

RELUCTANCE.—A measure of the opposition that a material offers to magnetic lines of force.

RESISTANCE.—The opposition to the flow of current caused by the nature and physical dimensions of a conductor.

RESISTOR.—A circuit element whose chief characteristic is resistance; used to oppose the flow of current.

ELECTRICAL TERMS AND FORMULAS

RETENTIVITY.—The measure of the ability of a material to hold its magnetism.

RHEOSTAT.—A variable resistor.

SATURABLE REACTOR.—A control device that uses a small d-c current to control a large a-c current by controlling core flux density.

SATURATION.—The condition existing in any circuit when an increase in the driving signal produces no further change in the resultant effect.

SELF-INDUCTION.—The process by which a circuit induces an e.m.f. into itself by its own magnetic field.

SERIES-WOUND.—A motor or generator in which the armature is wired in series with the field winding.

SERVO.—A device used to convert a small movement into one of greater movement or force.

SERVOMECHANISM.—A closed-loop system that produces a force to position an object in accordance with the information that originates at the input.

SOLENOID.—An electromagnetic coil that contains a movable plunger.

SPACE CHARGE.—The cloud of electrons existing in the space between the cathode and plate in a vacuum tube, formed by the electrons emitted from the cathode in excess of those immediately attracted to the plate.

SPECIFIC GRAVITY—The ratio between the density of a substance and that of pure water, at a given temperature.

SYNCHROSCOPE—An instrument used to indicate a difference in frequency between two a-c sources.

SYNCHRO SYSTEM.—An electrical system that gives remote indications or control by means of self-synchronizing motors.

TACHOMETER.—An instrument for indicating revolutions per minute.

TERTIARY WINDING.—A third winding on a transformer or magnetic amplifier that is used as a second control winding.

THERMISTOR.—A resistor that is used to compensate for temperature variations in a circuit.

THERMOCOUPLE.—A junction of two dissimilar metals that produces a voltage when heated.

TORQUE.—The turning effort or twist which a shaft sustains when transmitting power.

TRANSFORMER.—A device composed of two or more coils, linked by magnetic lines of force, used to transfer energy from one circuit to another.

TRANSMISSION LINES.—Any conductor or system of conductors used to carry electrical energy from its source to a load.

VARS.—Abbreviation for volt-ampere, reactive.

VECTOR.—A line used to represent both direction and magnitude.

VOLT.—The unit of electrical potential.

VOLTMETER.—An instrument designed to measure a difference in electrical potential, in volts.

WATT.—The unit of electrical power.

WATTMETER.—An instrument for measuring electrical power in watts.

Formulas

Ohm's Law for d-c Circuits

$$I = \frac{E}{R} = \frac{P}{E} = \sqrt{\frac{P}{R}}$$

$$R = \frac{E}{I} = \frac{P}{I^2} = \frac{E^2}{P}$$

$$E = IR = \frac{P}{I} = \sqrt{PR}$$

$$P = EI = \frac{E^2}{R} = I^2 R$$

Resistors in Series

$$R_T = R_1 + R_2 \ldots$$

Resistors in Parallel

Two resistors

$$R_T = \frac{R_1 R_2}{R_1 + R_2}$$

More than two

$$\frac{1}{R_T} = \frac{1}{R_1} + \frac{1}{R_2} + \frac{1}{R_3}$$

ELECTRICAL TERMS AND FORMULAS

R-L Circuit Time Constant equals

$$\frac{L \text{ (in henrys)}}{R \text{ (in ohms)}} = t \text{ (in seconds)}, \text{ or}$$

$$\frac{L \text{ (in microhenrys)}}{R \text{ (in ohms)}} = t \text{ (in microseconds)}$$

R-C Circuit Time Constant equals
R (ohms) X C (farads) = t (seconds)
R (megohms) x C (microfarads) = t (seconds)
R (ohms) x C (microfarads) = t (microseconds)
R (megohms) x C (micromicrofrads = t (microseconds)

Comparison of Units in Electric and Magnetic Circuits.

	Electric circuit	Magnetic circuit
Force	Volt, E or e.m.f.	Gilberts, F, or m.m.f.
Flow	Ampere, I	Flux, Φ, in maxwells
Opposition	Ohms, R	Reluctance, R
Law	Ohm's law, $I = \frac{E}{R}$	Rowland's law $\Phi = \frac{F}{R}$
Intensity of force	Volts per cm. of length	$H = \frac{1.257 IN}{L}$, gilberts per centimeter of length
Density	Current density— for example, amperes per cm^2.	Flux density—for example, lines per cm^2., or gausses

Capacitors in Series
Two capacitors

$$C_T = \frac{C_1 C_2}{C_1 + C_2}$$

More than two

$$\frac{1}{C_T} = \frac{1}{C_1} + \frac{1}{C_2} + \frac{1}{C_3}...$$

Capacitors in Parallel

$$C_T = C_1 + C_2 ...$$

Capacitive Reactance

$$X_c = \frac{1}{2\pi f C}$$

Impedance in an R-C Circuit (Series)

$$Z = \sqrt{R^2 + X_c^2}$$

Inductors in Series

$$L_T = L_1 + L_2 \ldots \text{ (No coupling between coils)}$$

Inductors in Parallel
Two inductors

$$L_T = \frac{L_1 L_2}{L_1 + L_2} \text{ (No coupling between coils)}$$

More than two

$$\frac{1}{L_T} = \frac{1}{L_1} + \frac{1}{L_2} + \frac{1}{L_3} \ldots \text{ (No coupling between coils)}$$

Inductive Reactance

$$X_L = 2\pi f L$$

Q of a Coil

$$Q = \frac{X_L}{R}$$

Impedance of an R-L Circuit (series)

$$Z = \sqrt{R^2 + X_L^2}$$

Impedance with R, C, and L in Series

$$Z = \sqrt{R^2 + (X_L - X_C)^2}$$

Parallel Circuit Impedance

$$Z = \frac{Z_1 Z_2}{Z_1 + Z_2}$$

Sine-Wave Voltage Relationships
Average value

$$E_{ave} = \frac{2}{\pi} \times E_{max} = 0.637 E_{max}$$

ELECTRICAL TERMS AND FORMULAS

Effective or r.m.s. value

$$E_{eff} = \frac{E_{max}}{\sqrt{2}} = \frac{E_{max}}{1.414} = 0.707 E_{max} = 1.11 E_{ave}$$

Maximum value

$$E_{max} = \sqrt{2} E_{eff} = 1.414 E_{eff} = 1.57 E_{ave}$$

Voltage in an a-c circuit

$$E = IZ = \frac{P}{I \times P.F.}$$

Current in an a-c circuit

$$I = \frac{E}{Z} = \frac{P}{E \times P.F.}$$

Power in A-C Circuit
Apparent power $= EI$
True power

$$P = EI \cos \theta = EI \times P.F.$$

Power factor

$$P.F. = \frac{P}{EI} = \cos \theta$$

$$\cos \theta = \frac{\text{true power}}{\text{apparent power}}$$

Transformers
Voltage relationship

$$\frac{E}{E} = \frac{N}{N} \quad \text{or} \quad E = E \times \frac{N}{N}$$

Current relationship

$$\frac{I_p}{I_s} = \frac{N_s}{N_p}$$

Induced voltage

$$E_{eff} = 4.44 \, BAfN 10^{-8}$$

Turns ratio equals

$$\frac{N_p}{N_s} = \sqrt{\frac{Z_p}{Z_s}}$$

Secondary current

$$I_s = I_p \frac{N_p}{N_s}$$

Secondary voltage

$$E_s = E_p \frac{N_s}{N_p}$$

Three Phase Voltage and Current Relationships
With wye connected windings

$$E_{line} = 1.732 E_{coil} = \sqrt{3} E_{coil}$$

$$I_{line} = I_{coil}$$

With delta connected windings

$$E_{line} = E_{coil}$$

$$I_{line} = 1.732 I_{coil}$$

With wye or delta connected winding

$$P_{coil} = E_{coil} I_{coil}$$

$$P_t = 3 P_{coil}$$

$$P_t = 1.732 E_{line} I_{line}$$

(To convert to true power multiply by $\cos \theta$)

Synchronous Speed of Motor

$$r.p.m. = \frac{120 \times \text{frequency}}{\text{number of poles}}$$

GREEK ALPHABET

Name	Capital	Lower Case	Designates
Alpha	A	α	Angles.
Beta	B	β	Angles, flux density.
Gamma	Γ	γ	Conductivity.
Delta	Δ	δ	Variation of a quantity, increment.
Epsilon	E	ϵ	Base of natural logarithms (2.71828).
Zeta	Z	ζ	Impedance, coefficients, coordinates.
Eta	H	η	Hysteresis coefficient, efficiency, magnetizing force.
Theta	Θ	θ	Phase angle.
Iota	I	ι	
Kappa	K	κ	Dielectric constant, coupling coefficient, susceptibility.
Lambda	Λ	λ	Wavelength.
Mu	M	μ	Permeability, micro, amplification factor.
Nu	N	ν	Reluctivity.
Xi	Ξ	ξ	
Omicron	O	o	
Pi	Π	π	3.1416
Rho	P	ρ	Resistivity.
Sigma	Σ	σ	
Tau	T	τ	Time constant, time-phase displacement.
Upsilon	Υ	υ	
Phi	Φ	φ	Angles, magnetic flux.
Chi	X	χ	
Psi	Ψ	ψ	Dielectric flux, phase difference.
Omega	Ω	ω	Ohms (capital), angular velocity ($2\pi f$).

COMMON ABBREVIATIONS AND LETTER SYMBOLS

Term	Abbreviation or Symbol
alternating current (noun)	a.c.
alternating-current (adj.)	a-c
ampere	a.
area	A
audiofrequency (noun)	AF
audiofrequency (adj.)	A-F
capacitance	C
capacitive reactance	X_C
centimeter	cm.
conductance	G
coulomb	Q
counterelectromotive force	c.e.m.f.
current (d-c or r.m.s. value)	I
current (instantaneous value)	i
cycles per second	c.p.s.
dielectric constant	K, k
difference in potential (d-c or r.m.s. value)	E
difference in potential (instantaneous value)	e
direct current (noun)	d.c.
direct-current (adj.)	d-c
electromotive force	e.m.f.
frequency	f
henry	h.
horsepower	hp.
impedance	Z
inductance	L
inductive reactance	X_L
kilovolt	kv.
kilovolt-ampere	kv.-a.
kilowatt	kw.
kilowatt-hour	kw.-hr.
magnetic field intensity	H
magnetomotive force	m.m.f.
megohm	M
microampere	μa.
microfarad	μf.
microhenry	μh.
micromicrofarad	$\mu\mu$f.
microvolt	μv.
milliampere	ma.
millihenry	mh.
milliwatt	mw.
mutual inductance	M
power	P
resistance	R
revolutions per minute	r.p.m.
root mean square	r.m.s.
time	t
torque	T
volt	v.
watt	w.